# FROM DRAFT TO BOOK

# FROM DRAFT
# TO BOOK
## A Guide to Self-publishing

## KARA D. STARCHER

Mountain Creek Books
Chloe, WV

Copyright 2022 by Kara D Starcher
Mountain Creek Books
PO Box 93
Chloe WV 25235
mountaincreekbooks.com

Every effort has been made to ensure the content provided in this book is accurate and helpful at the time of publication. However, this book is not an exhaustive treatment of the subject. No liability is assumed for losses or damages due to the information provided. You are responsible for your own choices, actions, and results.

All website links were accurate at the time of publication.

ISBN: 978-0-578-35756-0
Library of Congress Control Number: 2022900960

Editor: Lisa Thompson
Cover Design: Josh Aul

31 30 29 28 27 26 25 24 23 22    1 2 3 4 5

*To my mother*
*for instilling in me a love*
*for words and books*

# Contents

## Part 2: Designing

## Part 3: Printing

## Part 4: Planning

# INTRODUCTION

*FROM DRAFT TO BOOK* is meant to be used as a guide and not a definitive bible of the self-publishing process. This book does not discuss marketing and advertising. The four parts—Writing and Editing, Designing, Printing, and Planning—cover basic information about each specific stage of book production. Read the book from cover to cover or only the sections you need. Part Three: Printing and Part Four: Planning are designed to work together. It was difficult to explain the choices necessary for planning without reviewing the basics of printing first.

Self-publishing has evolved considerably over the past decade, making it easy for anyone to publish a book. In fact, I'm going to assume that since you are reading this book, you are planning or thinking about publishing your own book. Not too long ago, you would've had to rely on a publishing house to publish your book for you. Many people dreamed of writing a book and becoming a published author, but very few achieved that dream. Thousands of manuscripts sat unpublished in slush piles, waiting for someone to choose the best of the best for a publishing contract. Once that contract was signed, the publishing house did all the work on the manuscript to produce the book. The publisher took care of the editing, the book design, the printing, and the marketing.

With the advent of self-publishing, the publishing house's tasks—editing, design, etc.—became the responsibility of the independent author (someone who is self-publishing without the benefit of a traditional publishing house). Authors were left to figure out how to do all the tasks themselves. Thankfully, veteran indie authors and service providers have put together various resources over the years to help guide new indie authors.

The goal of this book is to educate you, the author, so you can make informed business decisions about your book, not fall prey to the predators, and save money in the process. If you remember nothing else from this book, remember these two things:

1.  **If any part of the self-publishing process intimidates you, hire a professional to help you.** As an indie author, you could go it alone and do all the work yourself from the beginning of the writing process to the final upload of the book. And some authors are successful at doing just that. But for many, doing it all alone can be a lesson in frustration, time management, and expensive mistakes. Thankfully, just like we have independent authors out there, we have independent professionals called freelancers or service providers who specialize in various areas of book production. Don't be afraid to invest in your book and hire a pro to help.

2.  **Self-publishing is a learning experience, and every learning experience has its challenges.** When you encounter a challenge, take a deep breath. Don't overwhelm yourself. (See #1.) Be patient and don't rush the process. Rushing creates errors, and errors cost money. In the back of this book is a three-month plan for going from draft to book. Use it as a guide, but don't lock yourself in on the timeline.

# 1

# WHAT YOU NEED TO KNOW

THE WORLD OF INDEPENDENT publishing can be a scary, overwhelming place if you don't know what to look for and what to watch out for. Anytime you are considering hiring someone to help produce your book, exercise caution. Quite a few wolves in sheep's clothing are out there. What a company says might sound promising, but they want your money, and sometimes you can do better on your own as a true indie author.

I'm sure you've seen publishers brag about the increased availability of your book if you purchased their upgraded silver publishing package for an additional $1,000. They might say something like "Choose this package, and your book will appear on websites for Walmart, Target, Barnes & Noble, and dozens more." That's exciting, right? Who doesn't want their book available on those websites?

What if I told you it costs only $49 (through IngramSpark) for your book to be available worldwide on 40,000+ online retailer websites, including those mentioned above? (To learn more about IngramSpark, the largest book distributor in the world, go to ingramspark.com.) What if I told you that it might take a total of two to three hours of your time to set up an account, upload your book, approve the proof, and place your book in distribution to those 40,000+ retailers? That publisher's silver package for $1,000 doesn't sound so promising now, does it?

## Identifying Vanity Presses and Hybrid Publishers

IF YOU'VE SPENT ANY time in self-publishing social media groups or googled the process, I'm sure you've seen the term "vanity press." And the newer term "hybrid publisher" is now floating around. You need to be aware of these wolves.

A vanity press is a "publisher" (and I use that term very loosely) who charges an author a large sum of money, keeps the majority of book royalties, owns the ISBN, and generally does nothing to promote the book even though they promise the world when it comes to marketing. If you think a company might be a vanity press, run away. You will regret the day you wasted your money. A hybrid publisher is a publisher who offers traditional publishing contracts as well as a pay-as-you-go model for hand-selected authors. Not all hybrid publishers are bad news. Make sure you understand exactly what you are paying for and that you are getting the most bang for your buck.

If you suspect that a company might be a vanity press or a not-so-reputable hybrid, google the company name plus the word "review" and see what others have to say. Also, if the "publisher" contacts you either via phone or email and offers to publish your book, proceed cautiously. These offers are almost always expensive scams and connected to a vanity press.

The Alliance of Independent Authors (ALLi) has an excellent resource for checking whether a publisher or service provider is reputable. Note that it's impossible to include all publishers and providers on a single list. Beware if a company is marked with a cautionary or worse warning. Visit selfpublishingadvice.org/best-self-publishing -services/.

For an in-depth discussion about vanity presses and how to identify one, visit the Writer Beware® website: sfwa.org/other-resources /for-authors/writer-beware/vanity/.

# Finding Professional Service Providers

How DO YOU GO about finding professionals to help you on your self-publishing journey? First, read this book from cover to cover. Know what you need to do on your own to produce a quality book. Understand the costs involved in the process. Once you know and understand these points, search for vetted service providers who can help you. Ask for recommendations from other authors or check with professional organizations, such as the Editorial Freelancers Association (EFA) or the Alliance of Independent Authors, for names and qualifications of service providers.

Service providers might offer multiple services connected to publishing. And that's okay. A service agency is not the same thing as a vanity press or hybrid publisher. The service provider will not be listed as the publisher of the book and does not retain the rights to the book. For example, my company offers everything from big-picture edits to design to assistance with setting up accounts for printing. I know what my strengths are, and I refer authors to vetted colleagues for areas outside my expertise, such as proofreading. I am not involved with anything that happens after the creation of the final print files. The actual publishing of the book is the responsibility of the author.

Why do service providers offer multiple services? We recognize that the self-publishing world is a maze to navigate and that not everyone who hangs out a shingle is a professional. In addition, we don't want to see our clients taken advantage of by scammers and imposters who are out to make a dollar.

# Hiring a Freelance Service Provider

## Contracts

ALWAYS SIGN A CONTRACT. Don't agree to work with someone or pay them money without having a signed contract in place. Let me repeat that—Don't work with a freelancer or pay money without a signed contract. Why is the contract important? It acts as legal protection for both you and the freelancer, plus it spells out the details about the work.

The freelancer, not you, should provide the contract. The freelancer is running a business, and having a contract is part of doing business.

If the freelancer brushes you off about a contract, be skeptical. The lack of a signed contract puts you in a precarious position if unforeseen circumstances happen.

The contract should cover the following:

1. The scope of work (exactly what will or will not be done),

2. The cost of the work,

3. When payment is due,

4. Details about the deposit,

5. What the deliverable work will be (a PDF, a Word doc, source files), and

6. The deadline schedule or when you can expect to receive the final product.

### Nondisclosure Agreement (NDA)

Is an NDA the same as a contract? No. The contract is a legal document that spells out the terms of your working relationship with the freelancer. An NDA is an agreement that states a person will not discuss anything about your manuscript with anyone else.

Is an NDA necessary? While you might feel better about having an NDA, it is definitely not a necessity unless your manuscript contains proprietary information. In fact, most professionals in the publishing world, including freelancers and publishing house employees, shy away from NDAs because they simply aren't necessary. Some companies and freelancers, however, place a confidentiality clause in the contract. This clause generally states that the people working on the manuscript will not discuss the contents outside the normal work environment. So if you are concerned about confidentiality or proprietary information, check the service provider's contract to see if it includes a confidentiality clause rather than a separate NDA.

### Communication

After signing the contract, the freelancer should give you a timeline of when they will be in touch again. Professionals are individuals, and we all work differently. Some check in with their clients once a week; others disappear for a few weeks while they work on the project.

At some point before the service provider starts working on your project, make sure you—

- understand when and how the freelancer will communicate;
- have a way of contacting the freelancer in case an emergency happens on your end; and
- ask what their preferred method of communication is. Some are okay with texting; others prefer email only.

Why are those three things important? I recently read a story in a social media forum about an author who hired an illustrator. They met a few times via Zoom and went over the project together. Friends who had previously worked with the illustrator recommended her, and the author had been happy with the meetings. A couple of weeks went by, and the author started to panic because she had not heard from the illustrator. The author tried texting and calling the illustrator but never received a reply. In the forum, people responded and told the author to demand a refund of her deposit.

Should she demand a refund? Maybe; maybe not. The first question to ask is did the author sign a contract? If so, what does the contract say about deliverables and deadlines? Did they discuss when the author would hear from the illustrator again? Did the illustrator state that she responds only to emails (very common) or a certain form of communication? Does the contract state that the deposit is refundable or non-refundable (common)? Does the contract have a termination or "out" clause? If the author wants to terminate the relationship with the illustrator, what exactly does the author need to do?

All those details should have been spelled out in the contract, and the author shouldn't need to ask for advice in a forum. Please note that if you have truly been ghosted by a freelancer, it is okay to do what is necessary by law to recoup your financial investment. Follow the termination clause in the signed contract and consult with an attorney if this happens.

Part One

# WRITING & EDITING

# 2

# BOOK
# BASICS

BEFORE WE TALK ABOUT what happens after you finish writing your book, let's talk about the components of a book and where they come from. Here's an assignment:

- Pull five books off your bookshelf.
- Open them to the first page.
- Flip through the pages of each book until you reach chapter one.
- Now ask yourself: What is the same about the books? What is different about them?

You should notice that they all contain the same pages in a similar order. First is either a half title page (just the book title), praise for the book or a previous book, or the actual title page. Next comes the copyright page, dedication, table of contents, etc. A difference might be that some have a table of contents while others don't. And others might have an introduction or a preface or other material before the first chapter.

These pages in the front of the book before chapter one are called front matter. The pages in the back of the book after the final chapter are called back matter. Front matter contains the basic information about the book's contents, and the back matter contains references and additional details about the contents. Nonfiction books usually contain more elements in the back matter than fiction books and possibly include end notes, a bibliography, referenced works, and an index.

## Basic Book Elements

THE BASIC ELEMENTS* OF a book in order are:

| | |
|---|---|
| Title page | Main text |
| Copyright page | Author's note |
| Dedication | Endnotes |
| Table of Contents | Bibliography |
| Introduction | Appendix |
| Foreword | Acknowledgments |
| Preface | Author biography |
| Prologue | |

*Not every book will have all elements

## Writing the Front and Back Matter

AFTER WORKING WITH DOZENS of authors over the years, I know that most authors don't even think about compiling or writing any extra pages until the last minute. Some don't even realize that they needed certain pages. Others simply forgot or needed direction on what to include. And that's okay. Ultimately, the content of the front matter and the back matter are the author's responsibility. Sometimes an editor and even a designer give input on what should be included on a page, but the author is still responsible for writing or at least approving the content.

## Page Numbering for Front Matter

THE GENERAL RULE FOR page numbering is that the front matter of the book uses small Roman numerals (iv, v, vi, vii) and the main text uses Arabic numbers (1, 2, 3).

The Introduction can be numbered with either the front matter or the main text, depending on the contents. (Where to put the Introduction is a decision best made by you and your editor.) Not including the Introduction with the front matter means the last item numbered with the front matter is either the Preface or Acknowledgments.

# 3

# BOOK PARTS

IN THE FOLLOWING SECTIONS, we will review the front matter elements, the proper order, and who is responsible for writing each element. Hint: It's usually the author's responsibility.

## Title Page

EVERY BOOK NEEDS A title page. The author should compile this information and place it on the very first page of the manuscript.

For a professional look, request that your book designer reflect the cover design on the title page. At a minimum, the designer should be able to mimic the look (font) of the title.

### What information goes on the title page?
- Book title and subtitle
- Author name
- Publishing company logo—Not a necessity, but recommended.

*Do not include the word "by" before your name.*

For a professional look, request that your book designer mimic the look (font) of the title.

# Copyright Page

THIS PAGE IS ONE of the most important pages in the book because it contains technical information about the book. The copyright page does not need to be complete for the editing phase, but it should be assembled before or during the final interior page design process. The author is responsible for compiling the information and verifying that the entire page is accurate. Certain pieces of information may not be available until the last minute, and the page designer may insert that information. The author is still responsible for making sure anything inserted at the last minute is correct.

## What do you include on the copyright page?

1. **Copyright, year, and copyright holder's name**
   The copyright notice should be the first piece of information on the page. The notice looks like "Copyright 2021 Kara Starcher" or "© 2021 Kara Starcher." Some authors place the copyright symbol © between the word "copyright" and the date, but it isn't necessary. Choose one or the other, not both.

   Who is the copyright holder? If you are self-publishing, it is you, the author, not your publishing company. In certain circumstances, it would be appropriate to use the publisher name, but for most books, it will be the author. If you are using a pen name, it is up to you if you use your pen name or your real name as the copyright holder. In cases where anonymity is important, use your pen name.

   For more information about copyright and registering for copyright, see Chapter Twenty-Six: Copyright.

2. **All rights reserved statement**
   Underneath the copyright notice, you should place the following statement or a variation:

   "All rights reserved. This book is protected by the copyright laws of the United States of America. No portion of this book may be stored electronically, transmitted, copied, reproduced, or reprinted for commercial gain or profit without prior written permission from the author. Only the use of short quotations for reviews or as reference material in other works and occasional page copying for personal or group study is allowed without written permission."

3. **Publisher name and address**

This isn't a necessity but is recommended. Readers should have a way to contact the publisher if they want to use all or part of the book for any purpose outside of reading it.

As a self-publisher, you may not want to include your home address. Alternatives are to rent a US Post Office box or use a virtual mailbox service.

4. **Disclaimers**

Disclaimers are popular in some fiction genres and in nonfiction. Pick up copies of other books in your genre and see what, if any, disclaimers are on the copyright page. Some popular disclaimers state that
- the book is a work of fiction and the characters are not real people;
- the book is a true story but the names and places have been changed to protect the privacy of individuals; or
- the advice given in the book is not meant to replace the recommendations of a medical, legal, or financial professional.

5. **Permissions and other credits**

Here, you can credit your cover designer, editor, photographer, or any other person who helped with the creation of your book. You can name them on this page like this—"Editor: Kara Starcher, www.website.com"—and on the acknowledgments page you can write more about the individuals if you want.

If you quoted other material requiring a permissions notice in the book, typically include that notice on the copyright page. For example, a religious manuscript that quotes a certain version of the Bible would use a notice similar to the following:

The Holy Bible, Version name, Copyright year by publisher. Used by permission. All rights reserved.

6. **LCCN or CIP data**

    The Library of Congress Control Number (LCCN) or the Catalogue in Publication (CIP) data goes on the copyright page. See Chapter Twenty-Five: Library of Congress for more information.

7. **ISBN**

    The International Standard Book Number (ISBN) is a numerical identification number for a book. Every ISBN is unique and identifies one specific book. An ebook, audio book, paperback, and hardback will all have different ISBNs. The ISBN for your book must be placed on the copyright page. For more information about ISBNs, see Chapter Twenty-Four: ISBNs and Barcodes.

**TIP**

When publishing a book in more than one format (paperback, ebook, hardback, etc.), include all the ISBNs on your copyright page. Listing the ISBNs means you can use the same interior design file for both paperback and hardback without modifying the copyright page.

8. **Country of printing**

    If you use a print-on-demand service, you do not include this information on the copyright page because you do not know where each individual copy will be printed. For offset printing, you can include that the book is printed in your country or whichever country the print facility is located in.

# Dedication

A BOOK DOES NOT need a dedication page, but if you include one, it is up to you to write it.

# Table of Contents

IF YOUR EDITOR REQUESTS a table of contents, include it in your manuscript. Otherwise, a designer can create a table of contents in a matter of seconds during the interior page design process.

The current trend is to not include a table of contents in printed fiction books. The table of contents is a necessity for an ebook, no matter what genre, because the ebook navigation relies on the table of contents.

Another trend is to label the table of contents only as "Contents."

# Nonfiction Books

## Foreword

THE FOREWORD IS WRITTEN by someone other than the author. The person's name is included at the end of the Foreword. If the Foreword is lengthy, the writer's name can be placed in the beginning underneath the word "Foreword."

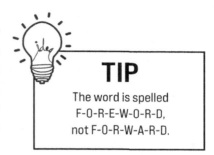

**TIP**

The word is spelled F-O-R-E-W-O-R-D, not F-O-R-W-A-R-D.

## Preface and Introduction

THESE ARE BOTH WRITTEN by the author, and sometimes it's hard to know which label to choose.

The Preface discusses the book as a whole, not the individual contents of the book. It can include the reasons why the book was written and how the material was gathered. If the acknowledgments are not a separate section, they can be included in the Preface.

The Introduction is about the contents or subject of the book. It may include basic information about the topic, explanations of terminology, or even a personal story by the author about the subject.

## Acknowledgments

THE ACKNOWLEDGMENTS CAN GO in the front or back matter. It's up to the author to write them and choose where to place them.

# Fiction Books

INSTEAD OF A FOREWORD, Preface, or Introduction, some fiction books contain a Prologue. The Prologue is related to the storyline and generally takes place at some point in time before the main story. The characters in the Prologue may or may not be the same as the ones in the story. The Prologue sets the stage for what the conflict may be.

If the Acknowledgments are included in the front matter of a fiction book, they are placed before the Prologue.

# 4

# AUTHOR BIOGRAPHY

Your AUTHOR BIOGRAPHY APPEARS in two places—on the back cover and at the end of the book. Some authors use the same biography in both locations; others use a short biography on the back cover and a longer one at the end of the book. The choice is yours.

How short is short? Twenty-five to one hundred words. Aim for either one or two concise sentences. The smaller the trim size of your book, the shorter the biography should be. The short bio should be fun and informative.

How long is long? One hundred to three hundred words.

## What is included in a biography?

### Prior publications
Any PREVIOUSLY PUBLISHED BOOKS should be mentioned but keep the list short. The general rule of thumb is to list three titles or less.

### Higher education degrees
INCLUDE YOUR DEGREES ONLY if relevant to your book topic. If you are

writing contemporary romance, your readers probably won't care that you have a PhD in psychology, but if you are writing a nonfiction book about relationships, the PhD qualifies you to speak on the topic.

## Awards and achievements

IF YOU RECEIVED AWARDS for your writing or made it on a list, such as *The New York Times* Bestseller list, include that information.

## Personal information

SOME AUTHORS LIKE TO include the state they live in, how many children they have, their job title (if other than a writer), and any unique hobbies. If you struggle with what personal information to include, pick something that you mention occasionally on social media or think about what you would want to know about someone else. Your goal is to make yourself personable to the potential reader.

## Website

INCLUDE YOUR AUTHOR WEBSITE at the end of both biographies.

# 5

# BOOK BLURB

WHEN IT COMES TO selling books, the book blurb and the book description are second only to the front cover. While a cover visually hooks someone to look at your book, the blurb and description should seal the deal and convince the reader that they need to buy it.

## What's the difference between a blurb and description?

THE BLURB IS THE short summary about the book that goes on the back cover. The description is the sales copy used for the book's online listings. Can they be the same? While the blurb and the description can be the same, it is not really recommended.

## How long should each be?

THE BLURB SHOULD BE 150 to 250 words. If you are using a smaller trim size, such as 5x8, try to keep the blurb to 150 words or fewer. The book blurb can be longer, but remember that you want to engage the potential buyer and pique their interest, not give away all the book's contents.

The book description should be longer than the blurb. Aim for 650 to 700 words. You will use this description in your marketing, advertising, and sales pitches. Sometimes authors use the blurb and then add reviews or a short excerpt from the book to make the description longer.

Some online retailers ask for a short description in addition to or in place of the regular book description. The short description will also appear as the book summary in any print catalog listings. The description should be roughly thirty to forty-five words. If you are struggling to write a short description, consider preparing a one-sentence elevator pitch and using that.

## Who writes the blurb and the description?

MOST OF THE TIME, the author writes these pieces. If you struggle with writing these, talk with your editor, especially if you started with a higher level of editing. The editor may be able to finesse what you wrote or offer fresh copy. Another option is hiring someone who specializes in writing blurbs and descriptions.

When you finish writing a draft, you should self-edit. Self-editing means you go back over the draft and look for errors, plot holes, structural issues, and more. Some writers self-edit as they write; others wait until they finish writing a chapter or the whole manuscript. Figure out what works for you. I'm not going into the details of what to look for when self-editing because you can find dozens of books and online resources on the topic. However, let's discuss some of the programs available to help with self-editing and what to do after you finish editing.

# 6
# SELF-EDITING
## AND
# BETA READERS

AFTER FINISHING WRITING THE first draft of a manuscript, you should always self-edit. That means going back over what you have written looking for problems with the story, organization, grammar, sentence structure, and more. In years gone by, the only option for help with self-editing was reference books. Today, we have software that can aid in the process.

## Self-editing Software

A FREQUENT QUESTION IN author groups is what software is recommended for self-editing. Popular answers include Grammarly, ProWritingAid, and Hemingway, along with others. Nothing is wrong with using one of these programs to enhance the editing process. The danger comes when an author relies on the software to fix their writing and when they blindly accept the suggestions.

These artificial intelligence programs cannot understand context, writer's voice, or style choices. The software is programmed to flag occurrences of problematic words and phrasing. Once a word or phrase is flagged, the software suggests a solution. The user then has to decide whether to accept or reject that solution. The problem is the solution may or may not be accurate based on the context. Unless the user has a fundamental grasp of grammar and style choices, accepting a solution can cause a bigger problem than the one the software flagged. Here's an example using a previous sentence in this paragraph:

> Original sentence—The problem is the solution may or may not be accurate based on the context.

ProWritingAid flagged "be accurate based" as passive voice. But it's not passive voice. The basic definition of passive voice is that the subject is not doing the action of the sentence. For example, the ball was thrown by the boy. In that sentence, the boy did the throwing, but the ball is the subject. When an action is done to an object by something else, you have true passive voice. To make our example sentence with the ball active voice, flip it around—the boy threw the ball.

In my original sentence, "the solution may or may not be accurate" is not passive. There's no action in the sentence. It uses a form of the "to be" verb (which also includes *am, is, are, was, were,* etc.). "To be" verbs can automatically trigger artificial intelligence to flag the sentence as possibly passive. Now the user must decide whether the sentence truly contains passive voice and if it needs a rewrite. And, if the user lacks a good understanding of true passive voice, the sentence may cause more work than necessary.

Here's another example of a software problem:

In Chapter Sixteen: DIY Cover Basics, the words "grid line" and "grid lines" are used under the topic Rule of Thirds. Grammarly flagged some, but not all, occurrences of "grid line" and said it should be "gridline," one word. According to Merriam-Webster dictionary, the word is spelled as two words. If I would have accepted Grammarly's suggestion without checking the dictionary and not noticed the discrepancy of only some occurrences flagged, I would have created errors.

If you decide to use software to help during the self-editing process, please review some basic grammar rules and ask questions about things you don't understand. Don't blindly accept every suggestion. If in doubt, leave your original version and let your editor correct the manuscript.

And one more example of why an author shouldn't rely solely on self-editing software: At the top of page five in this book is a bullet point that says "have a way of contacting the freelancer in case an emergency happens on your end." During the final design phase for the book, I was adjusting bullet lists and decided to rewrite the first bullet point to avoid an awkward page break. After rewriting it, I read over the complete list and discovered an error in the second point. It said, "...in case an emergency happens occurs on your end."

Happens occurs? How did an error like that make it all the way to the final design? First, human error. Somehow, I missed it and so did my editor. Second, self-editing software limitations. I copy/pasted the text from that section to a new MS Word document. I turned on the grammar check in MS Word, Grammarly, and ProWritingAid. Guess what? Every single one missed the "happens occurs" mistake.

# Beta Readers

ANOTHER HELPFUL RESOURCE FOR self-editing is beta readers. They read an early version of a manuscript and give the author feedback. They are perfect for testing a book's marketability and for pointing out areas that do not make sense. They are not a replacement for a professional editor.

## What qualifications should a beta reader have?

BETA READERS DO NOT need qualifications other than having a love for reading and a familiarity with your genre. As a fantasy writer, you do not want a beta reader who has never read a fantasy novel. While that reader might give some general feedback, they might miss some critical issues with the world-building or the genre tropes.

## How many beta readers should I recruit?

HAVING TOO MANY BETA readers means sifting through conflicting opinions and advice; too few means risking not receiving feedback. About half of the beta readers will respond. If you recruit eight to ten readers, you stand a chance of getting a handful of responses.

## When should I use beta readers?

YOU SHOULD USE BETA readers after you have completed a few rounds of self-editing. The manuscript should be complete in your eyes. It may have some flaws, but that's why you are using beta readers.

## Should I ask beta readers specific questions?

SOME AUTHORS GIVE BETA readers a questionnaire to complete after they finish reading. Nothing is wrong with this approach. As the author, you have targeted information about specific parts of the manuscript. Other authors request that readers simply point out any areas that don't make sense and what they do and don't like.

## What about alpha readers?

ALPHA AND BETA READERS are similar because they both give feedback. The difference is an alpha reader reads the first draft (or a very early draft) of a manuscript. Ideally, alpha readers should have professional qualifications in your genre. They might be members of a genre-specific critique group or a published author or some type of professional in the industry.

## What happens after beta reading?

AFTER RECEIVING FEEDBACK FROM beta readers, review their suggestions. For some authors, that means doing extensive rewrites because the manuscript did not resonate with the readers. For other authors, it's making tweaks here and there. After you've implemented the feedback, it's time to hire a professional editor.

# 7

# INTRODUCTION TO EDITING

THE BIGGEST PIECE OF information you need to know about professional editing is standard definitions do not exist for each type of editing. If you were to ask a group of editors what a certain type of editing included, you would receive a variety of answers. The lack of consistency in definitions is kind of ironic because the publishing industry deals with words yet doesn't have an agreed-upon standard definition of editing types. Since these standard definitions are lacking, you, as an author seeking to hire an editor, must ask exactly what is included in the work you are paying for. (This applies not only to editing but also to other areas like cover design.)

Consider this scenario: Samuel is looking for a developmental editor to evaluate and work with the overall message or story of his 75,000-word manuscript.

Mary quotes him $5,000 for a developmental edit with an estimated timeframe of six to eight weeks. Joanne, also a developmental editor, quotes him $2,000 and a timeframe of three to four weeks.

Why is there such a big difference in the cost and timeframe? Is it wise to go with the editor with the shorter timeframe and less cost? Not necessarily.

If Samuel asked Mary and Joanne what their edit includes, he would find out the difference.

Joanne's quote includes reading the manuscript, leaving comments in the document about what does or does not work, and then writing a ten-to-fifteen-page editorial letter about the manuscript.

Mary's quote includes reading the manuscript, leaving comments about problem areas, demonstrating suggestions for reorganization or rewriting, making editing suggestions via Track Changes, returning the manuscript so he can accept or reject her changes, another round of Mary reading the revised manuscript, and also copyediting the manuscript so it is ready for a proofreader.

Based on those descriptions, which one is better value for the price tag? Mary's edit will include multiple rounds of editing and give Samuel a manuscript that is almost ready for printing. Joanne's edit leaves the bulk of the work up to Samuel, plus he will need to interview, hire, and pay a line editor, copyeditor, and proofreader after Joanne is finished.

Which would you choose? And why?

## MYTH

"I'm afraid to share my whole manuscript with an editor because they might steal my work and publish it." I've seen similar statements dozens of times in Facebook groups. I'm not going to say that this situation has never happened, BUT a professional editor is not in the business of stealing manuscripts. An editor makes a living editing. If they stole manuscripts, they would be out of a job rather quickly plus subject to lawsuits.

# 8

# HOW TO CHOOSE AN EDITOR

Do not choose an editor because they are the cheapest or because they have the nicest website. Choose them because they are a professional and they understand your vision for your book.

The author-editor relationship should be built on a foundation of trust and respect. The editor should show respect for the author's writing voice and knowledge of the subject matter. The author should trust the editor's training and experience, and they should work together like a hand in a glove. So how do you find that perfect editor?

## Ask for Recommendations

If you like a person's book and the person speaks highly of their editor, put a lot of weight on this recommendation.

## Review Credentials

Does the editor have a website? If not, tread carefully. While anyone can create a website, the lack of one could indicate that the editor is either brand new or is not a serious professional. (A Facebook page is helpful but is not the same as a website.) Check the editor's website for the following information:

- What genres does the editor specialize in? Choose an editor who specializes in your genre.
- What type of training does the editor have? Training includes college degrees, certificates, or certifications. If the editor lists a degree with no additional certificates or certifications, the degree should be in either publishing, English, or writing. Editors in specialized fields like the sciences often have degrees in that field and then add a certification or a certificate in editing.

# Interview

ALWAYS INTERVIEW AN EDITOR before hiring them. Ask questions about their experience and their process. (See below for specific questions to ask.) For higher levels of editing (anything more than a copyedit), I highly recommend speaking via video chat or a phone call. A one-on-one conversation will help you know if the editor understands your vision for your book. An interview will also allow you to get a feel for the editor, tell you if your personalities will mesh, and if you will have that hand-in-glove relationship.

## Questions to Ask

1. **Do you do all the work yourself or do you outsource?**
   Exercise caution if the work is outsourced. When an editor (1) passes your manuscript to another editor who completes the work and (2) the payment is made to the first editor who did not do the work, we call that outsourcing. Outsourcing isn't always negative, but make sure you ask for and approve of the credentials for any editor who will be working on your manuscript. In some situations, you might not have contact with the editor working on your manuscript, and you want to avoid those situations.

2. **What style guide do you use?**

   The style guide an editor uses will tell you how familiar they are with editing manuscripts. Book editing is governed by *The Chicago Manual of Style*. Think of it as the bible of book publishing. It contains all the rules and preferences for writing books. If an editor says that they use Associated Press (AP), MLA, or some other style guide, question whether they are familiar

**OUTSOURCING**

Most independent freelance editors do not outsource to others unless they are running a service agency. Those running an agency are upfront about how the process works. Referrals and recommendations are different than outsourcing as well.

with *Chicago*. One exception is the medical, scientific, and psychology fields. These fields have additional style guides. And if you are writing in the religious genre, the editor should be familiar with *The Christian Writer's Manual of Style*. Most style manuals have multiple editions, and the editor should be using the most recent edition. Note: The dictionary the editor uses is important too.

3. **Do you use Track Changes in Word or show your work in some way?**

   You should see all changes in your manuscript via Track Changes in Microsoft Word or Suggestions in Google Docs. You should not have to figure out what the editor changed in your manuscript. The exception to this is when the editor makes minor "silent changes," such as deleting double spaces without showing that change.

## Sample Edit and Manuscript Critique

IF YOU ARE CONSIDERING a copyedit, request a sample edit from your top three editors. The sample edit will show you whether the editor uses a heavy hand or light hand and their overall style of editing. To effectively evaluate editors, provide all three editors with the same section from the middle of the manuscript. Compare their suggestions and decide which editor you like the best.

Not all editors offer free sample edits. Editing takes time; requesting a free sample edit is the equivalent of asking a mechanic to change a tire on your vehicle before deciding whether you will allow the mechanic to do other work on the vehicle.

For developmental editing or line editing, start with a manuscript critique. Since most critiques cost money, request one from your top choice. If you don't like the critique and suggestions, perhaps that editor is not the right fit for your manuscript, and it's time to choose another editor. Sometimes it's hard to determine via an interview if an editor understands your vision for the manuscript. A critique will erase any doubts you might have.

# 9
# TYPES OF EDITING

THE BIGGEST MISCONCEPTION ABOUT editing is that editing is identical to proofreading. Oh, my friend, there is so much more to editing. Proofreading is the final stage of editing that happens just before the book is printed. Prior to proofreading, books can go through multiple types of editing. This section reviews those types. Remember, different editors describe the types differently, so ask your editor exactly what they do or do not do for each type of edit.

The explanations of the types include a description, an approximate timeframe, and an investment. The descriptions I use are broad in order to give a general overview of each type of editing. The timeframes start once the editor begins working on the manuscript. Some editors might have a full calendar for a week to six months out, so even though a proofread only takes a week, you may need to wait eight weeks before the proofreading is complete. Always confirm the editor's availability and when you can expect to receive the finished edit. The timeframes will also be affected by manuscript length. A shorter manuscript will not take as long as one that is 125,000 words. When giving timeframes in this book, I used a manuscript length of approximately 75,000 words.

# Manuscript Critique

IF YOU ARE UNSURE of the type of editing your manuscript needs or if you aren't ready for an in-depth edit, a manuscript critique might be the right choice for you. A critique is also called an evaluation or assessment. See, sometimes we editors don't even agree on what to call a certain service!

The editor reads your entire manuscript through the eyes of a reader and an editor. The editor writes an editorial letter (also called a report) that reviews basic elements, such as plot, structure, organization, idea/character development, grammar, market, and audience, etc. The editor may or may not make comments directly in the manuscript. The report gives action steps to improve the manuscript and recommendations for the type of editing to consider in the future.

### How long does it take?

MOST CRITIQUES CAN BE finished within two weeks. That timeframe depends on the editor's schedule and availability.

### What is the investment?

FOR 75,000 WORDS, A critique will cost from $600 to $900 or more.

# Developmental Editing/Substantive Editing

DEVELOPMENTAL EDITING AND SUBSTANTIVE editing are big picture edits. Have you ever flown in a plane and looked out the window at the ground? You might see roads, buildings, fields, and lakes, but the details are obscure. You can't really tell how many windows are in a house or what make of car is sitting in the driveway. But the overall landscape is colorful and blends to paint a beautiful picture. A developmental edit looks out the plane window from ten thousand feet up to ensure a manuscript makes sense overall. For fiction, the editor looks at plot and character development; for nonfiction, the editor looks at organization and flow.

In general, the difference between a developmental edit and a substantive edit is what stage the manuscript is in. The developmental edit helps the manuscript cross the finish line. Maybe 50% of the manuscript is written, but wrapping it up is a struggle—that's where a developmental edit comes in. The editor works with the author to finish the story and to make sure all the parts make sense. This type of edit might mean deleting sections or scenes and adding others.

The substantive edit is identical to a developmental edit, but the manuscript is 100% done in the writer's eyes when they send the manuscript to the editor. Both edits focus on the chapters and paragraphs and whether they make sense within the context of the whole book.

## How long does it take?
DEPENDING ON THE MANUSCRIPT word count, this type of edit can take six to ten weeks.

## What is the investment?
DEVELOPMENTAL EDITING IS THE most expensive type. Pricing depends on exactly what the editor considers developmental editing and what type of feedback is provided to the author. In general, the cost may be five cents per word or more. For a 75,000-word manuscript, that would be about $3,750.

# Line Editing

LINE EDITING FOCUSES ON the individual sentences or the lines within a paragraph. The editor evaluates whether the sentence fits within the paragraph or if it would be better in a different paragraph. The editor also looks at overall word choice and may make suggestions for tightening wordiness or deleting repetitive words.

Some editors combine line editing with the developmental or substantive edit, and they do not charge for it as a separate service. Others combine it with copyediting (see below).

## How long does it take?
LINE EDITING TAKES FROM four to six weeks.

## What is the investment?
THE AVERAGE COST IS from four to six cents per word or from $3000 to $4500 for a 75,000-word manuscript.

# Copyediting

COPYEDITING IS THE TYPE of editing that most people think of when they use the word "editing." Copyediting looks at individual words and punctuation. These editors earn the nickname "grammar police." They will fix typos, misplaced commas, capitalization, spelling, word choice, and more. The copyeditor sometimes flags inconsistencies in facts and corrects word usage.

For nonfiction, if you use footnotes or references, confirm that the editor will check references and format footnotes as part of copyediting. Most editors charge extra for this service because verifying (or creating) dozens of notes and filling in missing information is a time-consuming process.

### How long does it take?

FOR A 75,000-WORD MANUSCRIPT, copyediting takes from two to four weeks. Shorter manuscripts will take less time.

### What is the investment?

THE AVERAGE COPYEDITING RATE is from two to four cents per word. A 75,000-word manuscript would range from $1,500 to $3,000.

# Proofreading

BEGINNING WRITERS SOMETIMES ASSUME that proofreading is the only kind of editing a manuscript needs. However, that assumption is wrong. Why? Because technically, proofreading occurs after the interior book pages are designed. The assigned proofreader reviews the actual page proofs, usually in a PDF, just before printing. Hence, the name PROOFreading.

A proofreader looks for errors in text alignment, page numbering, heading styles, minor typos, etc. The proofreader acts as the copyeditor's backup to make sure no grammatical details are missed. If you want someone to read your manuscript and fix grammar problems, you need a copyeditor, not a proofreader.

However, in some cases, a proofreader will check a manuscript before it goes to the formatter and designer. While this is not ideal, many indie authors are simply unaware that the book should be proofread as a PDF right before printing. Some proofreaders will check the final version in MS Word after the manuscript has been completely copyedited.

## How long does it take?

AN EXPERIENCED PROOFREADER CAN proofread a 75,000-word manuscript in one week or even less if the manuscript was properly copyedited.

## What is the investment?

THE AVERAGE PROOFREADING RATE is one cent per word or $750 for a 75,000-word manuscript. However, if the manuscript actually needs copyediting, the proofreader will charge accordingly.

# 10
# MONEY AND CONTRACTS

## The Investment

EVERY EDITOR WILL CHARGE you a fee to edit your manuscript. That fee is how editors make a living. If the fee an editor quotes is not equivalent to at least minimum wage or higher, ask yourself why the editor is not charging a livable wage and then run away. Editing is very much a "you get what you pay for" industry. Cheap rates mean shoddy work.

### How Editors Figure Costs

EDITORS ESTIMATE COSTS BASED on either a per-word rate, a page rate, or an hourly rate. Some editors give a project rate, which is equivalent to a word or page rate plus any administrative costs and extras.

Note that a page rate is not the total number of pages in your MS Word document. Because writers use different fonts and font sizes, the number of words per page can fluctuate. An MS Word document using Times New Roman 12 point font will have more words per page than a document using Times New Roman 18 point. So editors calculate a page rate based on the industry standard of 250 words per page. To

determine how many industry-standard pages you have, take your overall word count and divide it by 250. The answer is the number of pages the editor will use to calculate the cost.

If you want a ballpark idea of how much you will need to invest in editing, a per-word rate is the easiest to figure out. Simply take the editor's per-word rate and multiply it by the manuscript word count. For example,

$$51,341 \text{ words} \times .03 \text{ (copyediting)} = \$1,540.23$$

If that number is hard to stomach, remember you are paying the editor not only for their time but also for their expertise and experience. Editors with years of experience generally charge higher rates than newer editors. If you want to know where your editor falls on the scale, check the Editorial Freelancers Association rate chart. The chart gives the median rate, not the average, so your editor may charge less or more than the listed rates. Ideally, you want an editor whose rates align with the chart or that are a bit higher. If the rates are significantly less than the chart, run away.

**TIP**

Allow an editor to see your whole manuscript before they tell you how long it will take to edit the manuscript. If I ask a painter how much it will cost to paint my house, the first thing the painter will do is ask to see the house. The amount of time and effort to paint a cabin is different than a 12,000 square foot mansion. Manuscripts are unique, just like houses.

A quick note about hourly rates. Make sure the contract states exactly how many hours are included in the fee and what the finished work will include. If not, you might be burned. Let's say the editor quotes you $40 per hour and says the project will take twenty hours. A week into the project, the editor says they've already used up the twenty hours and they are only halfway through the manuscript. Now what do you do? Do you cough up another $800 hoping that will cover the remainder of the manuscript? Or do you accept a half-edited manuscript? And what happens if, two weeks later, the

editor says they have three more chapters and no more hours left? With a project fee, a per-word rate, or a per-page rate, you would've known upfront exactly what the cost was with no surprises along the way.

## Deposits

EDITORS OFTEN REQUEST A deposit before working on a manuscript. The deposit can be either refundable or non-refundable. (Check your contract.) And the deposit may be anywhere from 25 to 50% of the overall quote. Depending on the scope of work and the cost, some editors might request the full amount up front. The final payment for the project is almost always due before the editor returns the finished manuscript.

# The Contract

WE BRIEFLY MENTIONED CONTRACTS in chapter one. The contract is the legal protection for an author's working relationship with an editor. Don't balk if an editor asks you to sign one. Beware of the editor who does not ask you to sign or says it isn't necessary. In today's electronic world, e-mail correspondence is considered the legal equivalent of a contract, so some editors use e-mail agreements as a substitute. Personally, I would request a formal contract.

A typical contract should include the following information:

1. Your name and book details

2. Scope of work—Type of editing to be done plus an explanation of what is included

3. Cost

4. Payment schedule, including deposit information and when the final payment is due

5. Deadline for when the editor will return the manuscript

6. A termination or "out" clause—This clause protects both you and the editor if unforeseen circumstances occur. Perhaps the editor has a family emergency, or you realize the editor is not the right fit for your book. The termination clause will give

details about the non-refundable deposit and what type of notification must be provided.

7. Nondisclosure or confidentiality clause—Some authors request a nondisclosure clause, but this is not a necessity in every contract. See Chapter One: You Need to Know for more information.

Whenever you read a contract, mark any unclear areas. Then request a meeting (via Zoom, phone call, or email) with the freelancer to go over your questions. If something in the contract still seems sketchy, consult with an intellectual property attorney or a contract attorney. The attorney will read the contract and advise you as to whether anything is a red flag.

However, some points in a contract are meant as a protection for the service provider in case of non-payment. For example, some freelance editors include a clause in their contracts that states the editor maintains the copyright on the edited version of the manuscript until final payment is made. Once final payment is made, the copyright reverts to the author, and the author can do whatever they want with the manuscript. To some, this clause seems like a red flag. But it's not. It protects the editor and their work. The edited manuscript is not the same as the manuscript the author wrote. The editor made those changes and owns them until the author pays for the editor's time and knowledge to make those changes. Technically, the author is purchasing those changes from the editor as "work for hire." As long as the author follows the payment schedule and the editor is paid for making the changes, the author receives the edited manuscript and maintains the copyright. However, if the author fails to make the final payment, the editor has the right to hold the edited manuscript. So while the copyright clause may seem like a red flag, it simply protects the editor to make sure the final payment is received for the work they've done.

Think of it this way—have you ever had mechanical work done on your vehicle? When do they hand you the keys for your vehicle—as soon as the work is complete or after you pay the cashier? It's always after you pay. The mechanic hands the keys to the cashier, and the cashier hands them to you once your payment is approved. If you don't pay, you don't get your vehicle back.

# 11

# WORKING WITH AN EDITOR

Working with an editor can seem like an intimdating process to someone who has never worked with an editor before. It isn't. Your editor is there to help you, answer questions, and guide you through everything you need to know. The following is a basic overview of how the majority of editors edit digital manuscripts.

## Recommended Software

You can write your manuscript in any program of your choosing, but the program must be capable of exporting or saving as a DOCX file (Microsoft Word). Because MS Word is the publishing industry standard for editing, your editor will probably request that all editing work be done in MS Word.

Editors communicate with authors by using MS Word's commenting and track changes features. MS Word also has excellent add-on programs and tools that simplify and speed up certain parts of the editing process. Utilizing these tools helps ensure a manuscript is in the best possible shape for the money invested.

## What about Google Docs?

AH, THIS IS A point of contention within the editing world. Google Docs is attractive to writers because the program and its documents are easily accessible on any device. Plus, the program is free. Who doesn't love free? However, some editors adamantly refuse to use Google Docs, and others will work in Docs if necessary. Google Docs is a great tool for collaborative projects with back-and-forth edits and lots of shifting, re-organization, additional writing, and re-writing. While the higher levels of editing benefit from its collaboration features, Docs is not so great for copyediting because it lacks the add-on tools of MS Word. If your manuscript is in Google Docs, ask your editor how you should proceed. You may need to export it to an MS Word DOCX file or simply share your Google Doc with your editor.

## What about Scrivener?

SCRIVENER IS TOP-NOTCH SOFTWARE for book writing. In fact, that's what I wrote this book in. However, when it comes time to pass a manuscript on to an editor, the manuscript needs to be exported as an MS Word DOCX. While Scrivener makes it easy to structure a manuscript and move things around, it cannot track changes and lacks a comment function. If your editor has Scrivener, they may be willing to work on a Scrivener file, but chances are they will want the MS Word file.

# Track Changes

SINCE THE INDUSTRY STANDARD for editing is Microsoft Word and most editors will request an MS Word file, authors should be familiar with MS Word's track changes and comment features.

I'm going to explain how to use those features, but the screenshots I share may not look exactly like your screen. During 2020–2021, Microsoft revamped the track changes and comment features. After a significant amount of feedback from users, Microsoft rolled back those

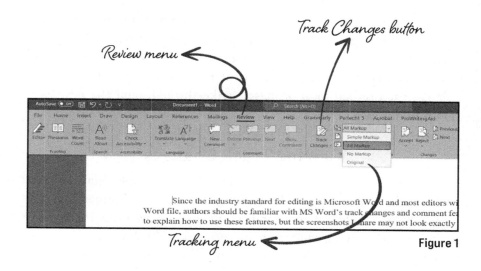

*Review menu* ←

*Track Changes button* ↗

*Tracking menu* ←

**Figure 1**

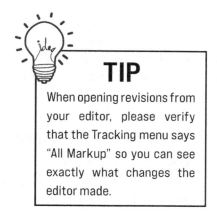

# TIP

When opening revisions from your editor, please verify that the Tracking menu says "All Markup" so you can see exactly what changes the editor made.

changes. MS Word also differs between the PC and Apple versions. However, even though the screenshots might look different than your screen, the basic idea behind the feature and the menu location of the feature is the same.

Under Word's Review menu, you will find the Track Changes button (see Figure 1). What does the button do? Turning on Track Changes means MS Word will mark every change made to a manuscript. Turning it off means MS Word no longer marks the changes. Tracked changes appear in a different color compared to the original text. (Note: Each user is assigned a different color, so your color might be green, and the editor's, red.) If a word is deleted, it appears with a strike-through like this: ~~deleted words~~. If a word is added, it is underlined like this: <u>new words</u>. If content is moved rather than simply deleted, the original location has a strike-through, and the new location is underlined.

## Viewing Track Changes

The Tracking menu contains four options—Simple Markup, All Markup, No Markup, and Original (see Figure 1). Simple Markup shows the revised text without indicating any changes other than a line in the margin showing where a change was made. All Markup shows the changes with the strike-throughs and underlines. It includes the original and the revised text blended together. No Markup is the revised text without any indications of where changes were made. Original is the original text before any edits were made.

The second menu under Tracking has options for which type of changes you want to see. I recommend turning off "Formatting" because those changes are generally not important and they clutter up the right margin.

## Accept/Reject Changes

Next to the Tracking menu is the Changes menu (see Figure 2). This menu is where you can accept or reject a change the editor made. Accepting a change means you like it; rejecting means you do not agree with the change and you want to keep the original text.

Under the Accept/Reject options are additional choices:

- Accept/Reject and Move to Next
- Accept/Reject All

Do not choose "Accept/Reject All" unless you have reviewed every change the editor made.

Some editors send two copies of the edited manuscript. One is the track changes version with all changes visible in the manuscript. The other is a clean manuscript with all the changes accepted. If you are overwhelmed by the number of changes, read the clean version first.

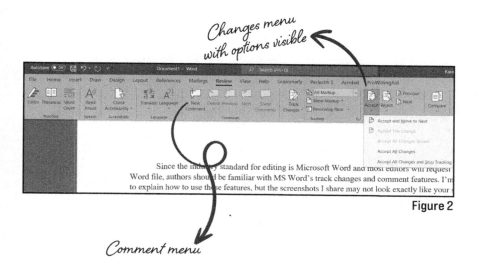

*Changes menu with options visible*

*Comment menu*

Figure 2

## Comments

COMMENTS, WHICH APPEAR IN the right margin, are where editors ask questions, explain changes, and make suggestions that are not reflected with track changes.

You have two options with comments. First, you can reply. If you are sending the manuscript back to your editor for another round of editing, replying to a comment is the perfect way to communicate your thoughts. If you aren't sending the manuscript back, you can leave notes for yourself as a reply.

Second, you can resolve the comment. When the author gives information, rather than asking a question or needing feedback, it's okay to resolve the comment. If the comment asks a question and you resolve it without answering, the editor will wonder what your thoughts were. Not too long ago, I came across this sentence in a manuscript: "You see, this is something that the children in the classroom rarely did." I highlighted the word "this" and wrote a comment asking what "this" referred to because it wasn't clear based on the context. Instead of replying, the author resolved the comment. On the next round of edits, I had to query the author a second time for the same word. And unfortunately, the author failed to answer the question again.

# Case Study #1

A FEW YEARS AGO, Amber contacted me and asked if I would help her figure out what was wrong with her manuscript. She had written a memoir focusing on a significant event in her life. That event led to numerous speaking engagements, and her audience wanted her to write a book. She shopped around for a literary agent for a few months, but before long, she accumulated a pile of rejections.

Most of the rejections didn't state why the book was rejected, but one did. It said, "No one will want to read this story. It's too sad." When Amber told me that, I hadn't read the manuscript yet, but I knew instinctively what the book was missing—hope. Her story needed to show the positive that came from the event.

I requested that Amber send me her manuscript, and we planned to do a critique followed by an edit. How big of an edit depended on what issues I found during the critique.

Overall, her story was well written. She was a natural writer. Very few flaws jumped out at me during my initial read. However, when I reached the end of the story, my first thought was "Where's the rest?" I scrolled up and then back down, thinking maybe more pages would appear. I opened Amber's original email, re-downloaded the attached manuscript, and opened that file. Maybe, I thought, I had accidentally deleted the last part of the manuscript. But nope, the new file ended at the same spot.

I evaluated the manuscript as it was, wrote my report, and sent it off to Amber with a request for a phone call when she was available. During the phone call, I explained reader expectations to Amber. She had told a beautiful yet heartbreaking story leading up to a tragedy that would bring even the coldest of hearts to tears. The problem was she left the reader at the tragedy. She never went into the details of what the next months and potentially years included. She didn't even talk about following seventy-two hours, let alone the week after the tragedy. The story literally ended within hours of the tragedy occurring. We talked about how to rectify that problem, which meant she needed to dig deep and write another chapter or two about a time in her life she would rather forget. We also discussed how to add the healing and the goodness that came from the tragedy.

The editing process was slow because the story was so emotionally charged. We worked on moving parts around to help the story flow cohesively. At one point, I sent some suggested changes to Amber, and I didn't hear from her. For an editor, sending big picture edits to an author is always filled with a bit of trepidation because we're working on the author's baby and sometimes rearranging the picture doesn't go over well. The next afternoon, I received a text from Amber—"Are you busy? Can I call you? We need to talk."

Uh-oh. This is not a good sign, I thought. As soon as I answered the phone, Amber said, "I need to apologize." I listened as she explained that she was angry when she received the suggested edits. She wanted to fire me and request a refund. How dare I change her book and her story! (At this point, I was stunned.)

She went on to tell me how her husband had talked her off the proverbial ledge the night before and told her to sleep on it before reacting. The next morning, she woke up, got her cup of coffee, and went on their deck to reread the revised version. She was still angry but decided to remain open-minded about the suggested changes. As she read through those chapters again, she realized it made sense and the story was better. Instead of telling events in a random order, they were now organized linearly, upping the impact of the story. She said the suggested changes were perfect, and she was thankful she had slept on it and didn't react in heat of the moment. Me, too, I thought.

About three months after I first read Amber's manuscript, her book launched with amazing reception. Within the first week, she hit #1 in numerous categories on Amazon and her book was in the Top-500 books sold overall on Amazon. Within a year, she had to do a second print run because she sold out of the ten thousand books she originally purchased to sell via her website and at speaking engagements. I often wonder what that literary agent who said no one would read the story thinks now.

## What can we learn from Amber's story?

- Flawed manuscripts are fixable.

- Utilizing beta readers and paying for a manuscript critique are perfect ways to find the flaws and boost the impact of your story.

- Receiving a critique and going through the editing process takes thick skin.

- Be open to changes and trust the professionals you hire.

Part Two

# DESIGNING

# 12
# INTRODUCTION TO DESIGN

Do you remember the saying, "Don't judge a book by its cover"? Guess what? It's not really true, because a lot of people judge books by their covers. Sometimes judgment is subconscious, and other times, it's intentional, but that judgment might mean your book fails to sell. And no one wants a cover that fails to sell. So how do you avoid that dilemma?

Hire a book cover designer. Other than editing, hiring a designer is the single most important investment you can make for your book. Note that I said a book cover designer. These individuals are specifically trained in designing covers. They're different than graphic designers. Some graphic designers overlap and create covers, but not all do. The same applies to the interior page designer. You need to hire someone specifically knowledgeable and trained in book design.

Before the design process starts for your book, you should have four things figured out.

1. **Editing**—All editing except proofreading should be completed before the interior page design starts. Proofreading takes place

after page design because proofreaders check certain elements of the design. If the editing is not complete and you decide to make changes after the book is in its final design format, you can create hours of unnecessary work for the designer. Something as simple as changing two words on page 59 can cause the next ten pages to reflow, which means the designer has to carefully recheck those pages. Those simple changes often translate into billable hours and a higher design cost for the author. So please make sure all editing is complete before entering the interior page design phase.

2. **Trim size**—This is the final size of your printed book. The most popular sizes for fiction and nonfiction are between 5.25x8 and 6x9. Your designer will need the specific size before starting work on the cover and the interior pages.

    How do you determine the trim size for your book? To determine the best size, check other books in your specific genre. Look at the top-selling books. What size are they? Check your bookshelves or go to the library or local bookstore. Take your ruler and start measuring.

    A novel works great as a 5.5x8.5, but a recipe book might work better at 7.5x9.25. What you don't want is for your book to be a different size (e.g., 5x8) than all other books in your genre (6x9).

3. **Color or not**—Will the interior of the book be black-and-white or color? This is an important detail because file creation can vary between the two. In addition, if you choose print-on-demand and want a couple of color images in your book, the entire book is priced as a color book. The costs for color printing can be astronomical compared to black-and-white, so make sure that those images are worth the cost.

4. **Print facility**—Your designer will need to know who will be printing your book so they can obtain any specifications from the print facility. See Printing Options for more information.

# 13

# DESIGN SOFTWARE

If Microsoft Word is the industry standard for book editing, what are the standard programs for book design?

## Adobe Creative Cloud

Adobe Creative Cloud is the most popular suite of software for designing print books. This suite contains the software that the major publishers use to produce books. Within the suite are some programs you may have heard of—Photoshop, Illustrator, and InDesign. Each of these programs has a separate function in the design process:

### Photoshop

Photoshop is ideal for creating a front cover or an ebook cover. Photoshop is photo manipulation software and allows images to be altered, blended, filtered, and so much more.

### InDesign

InDesign is the backbone of book design. This is the layout software that designers use to make a manuscript look like a book. The text on the page can be manipulated down to the character level to create an eye-pleasing page. InDesign is also the preferred program for creating the full, wraparound cover.

Ideally, when you are searching for a designer, you want someone who creates custom layouts (unique for your book) and uses InDesign. If you want to tackle learning the programs on your own, the Adobe programs are available via a monthly subscription. However, the programs have a steep learning curve. I say that as someone who has used InDesign and its predecessor, Adobe PageMaker, for over twenty years, and I still don't know all the ins and outs of the program. Because time is money in any type of business, including the book business, weigh your options and consider whether you can effectively and efficiently learn the software and produce a well-designed book.

If you decide to tackle learning an Adobe program, utilize the help section and the video tutorials on the Adobe website. The tutorials are in-depth, practical, and simple to follow. A helpful book is *Book Design Made Simple* by Fiona Raven and Glenna Collett. It illustrates how to create a book using InDesign and how the decisions you make affect the final book design. Note that the book is from 2017 so the illustrations are not from the current version of InDesign. Some menus and functions may not match the book's illustrations exactly. However, the book is still a valuable learning tool.

## Illustrator

ILLUSTRATOR IS ILLUSTRATION SOFTWARE for artists who want to draw digital images or manipulate typography. When creating color illustrations for a children's book, an artist will probably use Illustrator as part of their process.

If you don't want software with a steep learning curve, what other options are there?

# Affinity Publisher

AFFINITY PUBLISHER IS A software suite similar to Adobe Creative Cloud. It is a viable option to the Adobe programs and available for a onetime purchase versus a monthly subscription. I have not used the software personally, but my understanding is that there are some limitations as to what can and can't be done to text when compared to Adobe. However, Affinity is a solid option for someone learning the basics of book design who does not want a monthly subscription cost or to feel overwhelmed by Adobe programs.

## Atticus

ATTICUS IS A RECENT development in book design that I've heard promising things about. It offers both word processing and design within the same software program. An author could write a book in the program and then design it as well without having to import/export between programs. It's a onetime fee with no limit on the number of print and ebook files. As a web-based program, it is available for both PC and Mac as well as smartphones and tablets. A comparison of its features versus Vellum (mentioned below) is available on the Atticus website.

## Microsoft Word

IF YOU HAVE NO other options, you can format your book for print using Word. Remember, MS Word is a word processing program, not a layout program. It does not offer the detailed control over design that the other programs do. However, some people have excellent success using MS Word for book layout.

## Vellum

VELLUM IS TEMPLATE-BASED BOOK design software for creating both ebooks and print books. Because the software uses templates, the layout options aren't as customizable as InDesign, but the final product still looks professional. There's also an option for creating box sets if you write book series.

Vellum is available as a onetime purchase. You can use the software indefinitely without paying until you are ready to generate your final files. At that point, you can purchase the ebook-only version or the ebook and print version.

One caveat: Vellum is for Mac only. The software is not available for PC users unless they use Mac-in-Cloud to access Vellum.

If Vellum interests you, I recommend picking up a copy of *For-mat Your Book with Vellum: A simplified Vellum tutorial with notes for PC users* by Jody Skinner. She uses images and step-by-step instructions to guide readers from start to finish in creating a book. Plus she has a section specifically for PC users and how to access Vellum.

## Book Builders

MOST OF THE POPULAR print-on-demand printers offer some type of online book-buiding tool. These programs are not without limitations, so be sure to read all the documentation first. You will have greater control over the look of your book if you use one of the previously men-tioned software programs rather than a book builder.

# 14
# ELEMENTS OF PAGE DESIGN

IF YOU CHOOSE TO tackle your book page design yourself or if you want to verify that your page designer did the job correctly, you need to know ten basic areas of book design. Unfortunately, the detailed ins and outs of interior page design for print books* are too numerous to cover in this book. But knowing the tips in the following sections will put you well on your way to creating visually pleasing books.

*Print book design and ebook design are two different animals. Ebooks look different, depending on what device they are viewed on. If you plan to publish an ebook only, you can skip this chapter. However, do not try to create an ebook without studying the basics. For first-time ebook creation or for those struggling to create ebooks, consider using a program like Vellum. The results will be much better than winging it on your own. Trust me, I've tried both ways, and I had fewer headaches when I used Vellum.

## Page Size

THE PAGE SIZE SHOULD be identical to your trim size (the final size of a book when it is printed and bound). If your trim size is 5.25x8, the page size should be 5.25x8. No more, no less. The exception to this is if your book has images that go to the very edge of the page with no visible white space on the edges. Think children's picture books or full-color coffee-table books. In this situation, you will need to add "bleed" to the page size. The typical bleed amount is .125 inches on the outer edges; however, always verify with your print facility exactly how much bleed is required.

## Margins

MINIMUM PAGE MARGINS ARE .5 inches all the way around. Depending on the page count of the book, the inside margin (at the center of the book along the spine) may need to be larger. Personally, I use a visual margin of .5 inches for the top and bottom and .75 inches for the inside and outside. The larger inside margin helps with readability so the text doesn't curl toward the center.

Did you notice that I said "a visual margin of .5 inches"? That's different than the actual margin set within the document. Because I use InDesign to design books, my margin setup is slightly different than someone using MS Word. InDesign utilizes "parent pages" (formerly called "master pages"). I can place an element on a parent page, and that element will appear on any page in the book that I assign the parent to. When I create a new book that has headers and footers, I make my top and bottom margins .875 inches, not .5 inches. Then on my parent pages, I place the header and footer at the .5 inches mark. So visually, the margins around the page are .5 inches, but the actual text margin is .875 inches.

## Fonts

To CREATE A COHESIVE and professional look, use the fonts used on your book cover.

The main text of the book should be a serif font, which is a font with the letters with the little lines. Serif fonts are known for their readability and are the most common type of fonts used in books. Some examples are Garamond, Caslon, and Palatino.

Children's picture books are the exception to the serif font rule.

Since the goal for a children's book is to create a visually pleasing page enhanced by artwork, a sans serif font might work better in the overall design.

## Size

BECAUSE ALL FONTS ARE different, I can't recommend a specific font size as the best size for book text. For an example of sizing differences, look at the examples on the next page.Most fonts for text can typically be set somewhere between 10.5 and 12 points and be readable without being too small or too big. (This book uses Adobe Caslon Pro 11.5 point.)

If you wonder about a size, set up a couple of pages. Then print a copy, making sure it prints at 100% and isn't set at a smaller percentage. Compare the printed copy to some books on your shelf. Is your type smaller or larger? Adjust and reprint until you get the look you want for your book.

## Leading

THE LEADING IS THE space between

## LICENSING

Any font you choose must have the ability to be embedded in the final file for printing and must have a commercial license. Most, but not all, fonts that come pre-loaded on a computer can be embedded. Some downloadable free fonts are iffy for both embedding and commercial licensing. Before embedding a free font, you might need to purchase a commercial license. See Chapter Eighteen: Final Print Submission Files for more information about embedding fonts and how to check if your fonts are embedded.

Companies that offer commercial licenses include Adobe, Creative Fabrica, Font Squirrel, The Hungry JPEG, and Creative Market. Always check the licensing guidelines before purchasing or using a font for commercial use.

the lines. The general rule of thumb is that the leading should be 120 to 145% larger than the font size. Those percentages break down as approximately 2 to 5 points larger than the font size. So an 11-point font would have a minimum (120%) leading of 13 points and a maximum (145%) leading of 16 points. However, 16 points is rather large for book text set with an 11-point font. Depending on the font, my choice would be 11/14 or, in other words, 11 points for the text and 14 points for the leading.

Adjusting the leading is a visual skill. Too much leading (16 points) decreases readability. Too little leading also decreases readability, and the ascenders and descenders (the tops and bottoms of letters) start to touch between the lines. Again, I recommend printing a few pages and comparing the leading to books on your shelf.

Here's examples of three popular book fonts and how they vary:

*All three columns are the same size and leading.*

### Adobe Caslon Pro 11/14

The leading is the space between the lines. The general rule of thumb is that the leading should be 120 to 145% larger than the font size. Those percentages break down as approximately 2 to 5 points larger than the font size.

### Palatino Linotype 11/14

The leading is the space between the lines. The general rule of thumb is that the leading should be 120 to 145% larger than the font size. Those percentages break down as approximately 2 to 5 points larger than the font size.

### Baskerville 11/14

The leading is the space between the lines. The general rule of thumb is that the leading should be 120 to 145% larger than the font size. Those percentages break down as approximately 2 to 5 points larger than the font size.

*This gap is the bottom of a "river," a vertical white line through the text.*

*Same amount of leading but an entire line longer*

*Notice how heavy this text looks compared to the others.*

# Header

THE HEADER IS THE white space at the top of the page above the text. Common practice is for the header to contain information about the book. The book title is placed at the top of the left-hand page, and the chapter title, at the top of the right-hand page. For fiction, you can use a combination of author name and book title. If a nonfiction book is divided into titled parts or sections (like this book), the part title goes on the left page, and the chapter title, on the right. Sometimes the designer may choose to place this information in the footer (white space at the bottom of the page) along with the page number—this is an acceptable stylistic choice.

The header should not blend with the page text. It should be separated from the text by white space (a blank area with nothing in it). Using a different font for the header is also an acceptable stylistic choice. Note the different font used in the footer of this book. When using headers, the header is not placed on the first page of a chapter or any other divider pages, such as Part One.

# Page Numbers

THE PAGE NUMBER IS placed in either the header or the footer, depending on genre. For fiction, the number goes in the footer; nonfiction page numbers can be either place.

If the page number is in the header, it should be on the same line as the book title, chapter title, or whatever book information is in the header. The page number should not be by itself in the header. If the page number is in the footer, it's acceptable by itself.

When a page number is part of the header, it's dropped to the footer for the first page of a chapter.

# Chapter Openings

THE PRACTICE FOR YEARS was to always start a new chapter on the right-hand page. It is now acceptable to start a new chapter on either the left- or right-hand page. However, a new part or section should always start on the right-hand page even if it creates a blank page on the left.

Place the chapter title about one-third of the way down the page. The title is followed by white space before the text of the chapter begins. To coordinate your interior book pages with the book cover, try using the title font from the cover as the font for the chapter title.

The first paragraph of a chapter can start with or without an indent. If you choose not to indent, consider using a drop cap for the first letter of the paragraph or small caps for the first couple of words.

## Indents vs. Double Return or White Space

NEW PARAGRAPHS SHOULD START with an indent for the first line. The amount of the indent can be anywhere from .25 to .5 inches, depending on the font size.

Do not use an indent plus white space. Choose one or the other. A double return or added white space is a common practice for some self-publishers in nonfiction genres and is used to boost page count. Ideally, you want to avoid using the double return because it screams that the page design is amateur and is not a solid design practice.

A double return before a subheading is acceptable. A better practice, however, is to use the "space before" or "space after" options in whatever software program you're using. (In MS Word, this is under the Layout tab.) This book uses "space before" set to approximately .25 inches.

## Images

ALL IMAGES SHOULD BE converted to grayscale and cropped to size before placing the image in the manuscript.* To do this, you will need some type of photo manipulation software. "Cropping to size" means that if the image will be two inches wide by three inches high on the book page, that's the size that the saved image should be.

If you have access to photo software, figure out how to lighten the overall photo. When ink hits paper, the ink makes images appear darker on the page than they are on a computer screen. If your photo software has the ability to lighten just the mid-tones, do that. Always take photos one step lighter than what your eye tells you they should be.

*If you hire a book designer, please do not edit or crop your photos. Give the designer your original images. Make notes within the manuscript about the specific placement of each photo and what the important elements are in the photo. For example, if you have a photo of a house with a barn and only the barn is important, note that the final image should be of the barn, not the house and barn.

## Widows, Orphans, and Runts

Say what? We're not talking about people here. Widows and orphans are single lines of text by themselves at either the top (widow) or bottom (orphan) of the page. A runt is a single word, two short words (like "it is"), or part of a word by itself on a line at the end of a paragraph. To the best of your ability, you want to avoid any of these in your book. For an example of a widow, look at the top of the next page. I intentionally left that line by itself as an example.

One exception for widows is that a single line at the top of a page is acceptable as long as the line is "full measure" or fills the entire line. The example line at the top of the next page is not full measure, plus it comes directly before a subhead, so it should be corrected. Some designers do not worry about orphans at the bottom of a page in order to maintain a square page—the bottom line of both left and right pages match without one page being shorter than the other.

Adobe InDesign, other design programs, and Microsoft Word all have settings to help eliminate widows and orphans. Even with these controls turned on, it's always best to visually check each page to make sure the page breaks are acceptable.

Runts are a little more difficult to control. The way to eliminate them is to adjust the kerning (space between the letters) of a paragraph. When the kerning is reduced, it often, although not always, creates enough space on the previous line for the word to jump up to the end of the line. However, too much kerning will be noticeable because the paragraph will appear darker on the page than paragraphs without kerning. Tight kerning also makes words more difficult to read.

For an example of kerning, look at the chapter titles in this book. In order to make the title appear like a block with even edges, I adjusted the kerning between the letters. Sometimes I added kerning, creating the large white spaces. Other times I reduced the kerning amount so the letters appear to be tighter together.  *Widow*

# Page Depth

THE PAGE DEPTH IS the square created by the text on both the left and right pages. The depth should be even across the bottom of the page. That means the bottom line on the left page should match the bottom line on the right page. The exception is the final page of a chapter, which does not have to match the page next to it. Page depth is important because when you are correcting widows and orphans, the bottom of the pages might become uneven. InDesign has controls to manually adjust page depth, but MS Word does not.

# PDF Proofs

ONCE YOU ARE SATISFIED with your page design on screen, create a PDF of the interior pages. To visually proof the book, use the spreads option for the PDF. This will place the book pages side-by-side exactly how they will print. Open the PDF in a program like Acrobat Reader and zoom out to either 50% or 75% so you can see both pages in their entirety. Flip through the pages looking for any of the ten things on the list that you may have missed. And trust me, it's easy to miss a widow or a header on a chapter opener.

After you proof the PDF or receive it back from a proofreader, create another PDF according to the print facility specifications. Most want the PDF as pages, not spreads, with only one page showing at a time.

The type of PDF will be different, depending on where your book will be printed. IngramSpark requires a PDFx1a:2001 while KDP requires a Press Quality PDF. You can use the same interior design file to create the PDFs, but you might need to make separate PDFs.

**TIP**

KDP accepts PDFx1a:2001 files, but IngramSpark will not accept a Press Quality PDF. The PDF will upload, but it will return random errors during the validation process.

# 15

# COVER DESIGN

WHEN IT COMES TO book sales, the front cover design is perhaps the single most important part of a book. The book blurb shares a part in the sale, but the cover is the first thing a potential buyer sees. The cover is what intrigues the buyer to turn the book over and read the blurb. And the blurb seals the deal.

A book cover is literally the book's face. That face will appear everywhere—in advertising, on marketing materials, in online listings, and on social media. So it's in your best interest to make sure your book has an appealing face for its target audience.

How do you make sure that your book cover is the best it can possibly be? Hire a professional cover designer. Employing a designer is one of the two best things you can do for your book. (The other is hiring an editor.) If you cannot afford to hire a cover designer, carefully read Chapter 16: DIY Cover Basics.

## Investment

COVER DESIGN IS HARD to put an exact price tag on. For budget purposes, plan on $400–$800 for a full custom cover design. Some designers will charge less; some, more. I've seen well-designed covers for $75. I've also seen them for $800 and more.

Part of the price difference depends on the deliverables. If you pay $75, you might only get the front cover, which is perfect if you are planning an ebook only and not a paperback. If you are doing a paperback or hardback book, you need a full wraparound cover—front, spine, and back. Because more elements are involved with a full cover, the design process takes longer than for an ebook cover, so expect to pay more for the full cover. Another part of the deliverables is the print facility templates. Some designers include all the templates you will need, and others charge an additional fee for each template. (See Cover Templates in Chapter Sixteen: DIY Cover Basics for more details about templates.)

What about marketing materials? Will the designer provide 3D mockups of your book? What about promotional ads or individual design elements from the cover that you can use on social media? How about predesigned ads for social media? These extras add to the cost.

Just like with editing, it's important to ask the service provider exactly what is included in the price. That way, you can compare apples to apples rather than apples to oranges.

## Genre Expectations

BE AWARE THAT CERTAIN genres have expectations for not only storylines but also cover design. Not sure what I mean about genre expectations? Pull a couple of fiction books off your shelf or browse a book category online. What do you notice about the covers? Romance books usually have colorful, bright covers. The opposite is true for suspense or thriller books. Those covers tend to be darker with muted colors other than a pop of a single color like red or blue. Romance covers tend to have a couple on the cover, while suspense books might have an individual in the forefront with someone in the background. Historical fiction books feature the main character in period clothing. Make sure your cover matches your genre.

Warning: Don't try to be different and go against the norms of your genre. Don't create a dark, muted cover for a romance book. It won't work. Your sales will be negatively affected.

# Affordable Cover Alternatives

Now, what if you can't afford a professional cover designer? This is a major concern for many authors because a professional cover can be a big investment. Can you create your own cover? Yes, you can. But it's not recommended unless you have a background in art or design.

Time is money, and if you can find any possible way to pay for a professional cover instead of creating your own, please make that investment. I've lost track of how many Facebook posts I've seen asking for help with covers because the print facility is rejecting the cover. The solution almost always includes hiring someone to fix the original file. If you don't understand bleed or spine width or some other integral part of design, please hire a professional. You will save yourself a huge headache and time that could be better spent on editing or marketing.

**TIP**

KDP has an online Cover Creator tool that includes stock images and templates. You can use this tool to create your cover, but you cannot export or use the cover file anywhere other than on KDP.

## Premade Covers

Some designers who specialize in one or two genres supplement their income by creating covers ahead of time. They offer these premade covers for sale via their websites for anywhere from $25 to $100 or more. The less expensive covers are usually the front cover only and designed for ebook use, not print. The higher prices sometimes include the design of a full wraparound cover after you purchase the front cover. Once you order a premade cover, the designer will change the title and author name and make some minor adjustments before giving you the final cover file.

Ideally, you want a premade cover that comes with a onetime use guarantee so that no one else can purchase that same cover. The cover will be listed as out of stock on the website after you purchase it. Before purchasing a premade cover, review the licensing, terms and conditions, and also the deliverables.

To find a premade cover, search for your genre plus premade book cover. For example, if you write clean romance, you would type in "clean romance premade book cover."

### Reedsy and More

Another potentially affordable option is to commission a designer via sites like Reedsy, Fiverr, or Upwork. I used the word "potentially" because you will find prices on these sites that match independent designer prices. If you choose this route, pay close attention to two areas:

First, make sure the images used on your cover have commercial licenses. If not, you might find yourself in a predicament later on, be required to create new covers, and face even more serious consequences, including possible financial sanctions.

Second, if you plan to do both print and ebook, verify that the designer is creating a print cover and not just an ebook cover for the price. Print covers require a higher image resolution and have to be sized specifically to your book's trim size.

## Working with a Cover Designer

The best advice I can give you about cover design is to trust your designer. They are professionals who have studied the craft and know what works and what doesn't work in the book industry.

One of the first questions a designer should ask an author is what the book genre is. Genre is extremely important when it comes to cover design, and if a designer does not ask about the genre prior to giving a price estimate, that is a red flag. As with editing, you want a designer who is familiar with your genre. Knowing the genre also tells the designer who your book audience is. For example, if your book is middle grade fiction, the designer knows that the cover has to appeal to children, rather than adults.

Once you sign a contract, the designer should ask additional questions so they can understand your vision for the cover. Every designer approaches this process differently—some use phone or video interviews; others use forms.

Here's the questionnaire I send to my clients:

1.  **What is your author name?**

    This should be exactly how you want your name to appear on the cover. If you use a pen name, make sure the designer knows the correct name.

2.  **What is your book title and subtitle if using one?**

    If your book has a subtitle, please tell the designer in the beginning. Don't wait until they've designed a couple of covers and say, "Oh, by the way, I forgot to tell you, but my book has a subtitle." Adding a subtitle to an already created design often throws the design out of balance and creates more work for the designer than if they had known up front.

3.  **What is the book genre?**

    Sometimes a title doesn't exactly give away the genre. *Death at Night* says the book is probably in the mystery/suspense/thriller category; *A Love Connection* says romance category. But *Clueless* is more ambiguous and could be a mystery or middle-grade fiction or quite a few other genres. It's important to make sure the designer knows the exact genre of the book.

4.  **Do you already have an image for your front cover?**

    If so, it must be a personal photo or one that has a commercial license agreement. Occasionally, authors pick out specific images, such as a personal photo for a memoir or an inspirational photo, for their covers. Any stock photo is okay to use as long as it comes with a commercial license. Some websites offer free images with commercial licenses; other sites require a fee that can be as little a few dollars to more than $100. Because you will be selling your book, the commercial license must cover retail sales.

5.  **What objects would you like on your front cover?**

    Examples might include house, tree, church, road, city at night, beach umbrella, horse, or castle. The designer does not read your entire manuscript to find the important elements. You must tell the designer. If your main character always rides a black horse, specify that so that the designer doesn't put him on a white spotted pony.

Does your character have a certain physical characteristic that's important? Or do they always wear a certain item like a necklace?

This applies to nonfiction books as well. What objects or images represent your story? Do you talk about the four points of a compass and how they apply to life? Tell the designer.

6. **Do you have a color scheme for your cover?**

   This can be a single color or a combination of colors (pink/brown, red/black, purple/green, etc.) Color scheme tends to be more important for nonfiction authors, especially if they are building a brand. They want their book to represent their business and be recognized as one of their products. Communicate any brand details to the designer. Some authors, both fiction and nonfiction, plan out several covers in advance in order to ensure consistency for their book series or across their brand. When it's time to release the next book, the designer only needs to add the correct title.

7. **Is there anything you do not want on your cover, such as a specific color, fonts, or a certain look?**

   If you dislike certain colors, like pink or yellow, now is the time to tell the designer. Maybe you don't like those script fonts that resemble handwriting. Mention it. Maybe you don't like Stephen King's covers but love John Grisham's. Tell the designer. The more the designer can understand your thoughts and know your likes and dislikes, the better the outcome.

8. **What are your favorite covers?**

   Please provide links to at least three books that you feel represent the look you'd like for your cover. You might already have favorites you can send to the designer. If not, visit Amazon and search the top sellers in your book genre until you find some that catch your eye.

   These covers are called "comps" or comparables. Your book cover will be competing against these in the market. If necessary, you can choose covers from different genres, even though your book will not be competing against them. The designer is interested in what appeals to you and what catches your attention.

9.  **What do you like or dislike about each cover?**
    Please list the title, what stands out to you about the cover, why you like it, anything you don't like, etc.

    Sometimes authors struggle to verbalize why they like the cover. They just do, and that's okay. Other times, the answers are as specific as "I only like the title font, and I'd like to use it on my book" or "I like the texture used on the side" or "I like the colors but maybe not as bright and flashy." If you give the designer as many details as possible and can specifically point out what you like or don't like, the designer can most effectively replicate your vision for your cover.

After the interview, the designer will work on concept or sample covers. Some designers provide two or more concepts. Others start with one concept, ask for the author's feedback, and then build from there. Sometimes that means completely scratching the first concept, and other times, it means tweaking and revising the original concept. Either approach works.

When a designer shows you a cover concept, be open and honest about your thoughts. Don't be afraid of hurting the designer's feelings. The more feedback you give the designer about the concept, the easier it is for the designer to create a cover you will love.

# 16

# DIY COVER BASICS

If purchasing a cover is completely out of the question, here's what you need to know about creating your own cover.

## Full Cover

As I previously mentioned, a print book requires a front, spine, and back, not just a front cover. The full cover must be set up correctly in order for the cover to print properly. If you fail to set up the full cover correctly, some of the front cover may show on the spine or part of the spine might show on the back cover. Obviously, you want to avoid those things happening.

The full cover—front, back, and spine—should coordinate. It doesn't have to look like one continuous design, but the back cover should look like it goes with the front cover.

### How do you coordinate a front and back cover?
1. Use the same color scheme.
2. Pull graphics from the front cover to use on the back cover.
3. Use the same fonts.

# Cover Templates

MOST PRINT FACILITIES OFFER cover templates. A cover template is a blank document with the spine, safe area, trim lines, and bleed area marked. The cover template is created from your book specifications (trim size, page count, and paper choice).

The interior page design must be complete before requesting a cover template because a page count is required to accurately calculate the spine width. A 116-page book has a much thinner spine than a 378-page book.

Cover templates have a "safe area" marked. Anything within that area is safe from being trimmed off when the book is cut to size. Make sure all text and important elements are within the safe area. Most facilities include a slight margin around the safe area before the trim line and the bleed area, so include that margin when trying to center images and text on the cover. Read the directions on the template to learn more about the safe area, trim line, and bleed.

A cover template is unique to the facility that gave you the template. You can copy/paste your full cover from one template to another and then make some adjustments, but submitting the same template to two different facilities does not work. For example, if you submit an IngramSpark cover template to KDP, the KDP cover proof will show your cover shifted upward and to the right with a significant amount of white space at the bottom. Only the bottom half of the full cover will show on the cover proof. The shifting occurs because IngramSpark's template has a wide band of white space on the left and bottom while KDP's template has no white space around it.

## CANVA

Canva is an affordable option for creating ebook and print covers. However, setting up a full cover wrap for print can be more complicated than just an ebook cover. In the Resources section on page 163, I list a website that has step-by-step instructions for successfully setting up a KDP template.

# Bleed

BECAUSE COVERS ARE EITHER trimmed to size (paperbacks) or folded to size (hardbacks), all background colors and/or images must extend beyond the trim-size dimensions. If you do not calculate the bleed correctly, your cover will be rejected, and you will have to resize it. The amount of bleed is not standard, so different print facilities may use a different amount of bleed. Check with your print facility for the exact amount.

To determine the proper dimensions with bleed, add the bleed amount to the trim size. IngramSpark uses a bleed of .125 inches for all outer edges. (The inside edge along the spine does not need bleed because it isn't trimmed off.) IngramSpark's front cover dimensions, including bleed for a 6x9 trim size, would be 6.125 inches x 9.25 inches or (6 inches wide + .125 inches bleed on the right side) + (9 inches tall + .125 inches bleed on the top + .125 inches bleed on the bottom).

# Images

ALL COVER IMAGES, NO matter how big or small, need to be in CMYK format. Covers are printed in color, and CMYK breaks the image down into the four basic ink colors. Computer monitors use RGB, which is only three colors. If you add the fourth color (CMYK) to a three-color image (RGB) that was not converted properly, the colors will not process correctly and will print differently than what you see on your screen. Using CMYK will give you the best visual representation of how the images and colors will look when printed. If you forget and fail to convert your images, your final cover file may be rejected by the print facility.

One of the downfalls of creating covers on a screen and then printing them is that colors are more muted when printed. If you want bright, vibrant colors on your cover, such as fire-engine red or fluorescent green, do your research on how to create those colors or work with a designer. Do not rely on how the color looks on your screen. Designers use monitors and software calibrated for print, and they know how to manipulate and choose colors for the best outcome. The last thing you want is for your fire-engine red cover to print as washed-out orange.

Because ink saturates paper, colors not only lose vibrancy but also print darker than what appears on a screen. The details in the shadow areas of a photo must be lightened so that they are visible when printed. Programs like Photoshop can help manipulate photos for the best outcome.

# Readability

READABILITY COVERS TWO AREAS. First, the fonts for the title should have standard letter formation. It's okay to use script fonts or some other type of fancy font as long as the letters are distinguishable. Potential buyers don't want to struggle to decipher a book title.

Second, the title should be readable when the cover is reduced to thumbnail size or approximately one inch high. Thumbnails are used on websites like Amazon, Books-a-Million, and Barnes & Noble. To check readability, zoom out to approximately 15–20%. Not every word has to be readable at that level, but the keywords in your title should stand out. For example, for this book's cover, I made sure that "draft" and "book" were readable when I zoomed out.

# Contrast

CONTRAST IS A BASIC graphic design rule. If you want something to stand out, use contrast. Think about black and white. What are they? Opposites. They contrast with each other. When you are choosing colors for your cover, look for contrasts. If your background, whether part of an image or a color block, is light, choose a dark color for the title. If the background is dark, use a light color.

Contrast also applies to size. Tall and short. Skinny and wide. Use contrast when choosing the fonts for your cover. Besides serif and sans serif, look for a heavy font with thick letters and a lighter font with thinner lines.

# Rule of Thirds

THE RULE OF THIRDS is used in photography and graphic design. The basic idea is to not place the main subject of an image in the exact center of the canvas. Instead, place the subject slightly to the left or right or slightly up or down.

When using the rule of thirds, the canvas (whether a photo, computer screen, or artboard) is divided by grid lines. The grid resembles a game of tic-tac-toe with nine squares and is made up of three even columns with three even rows in each column. Perhaps you've seen an option on your cell phone camera or digital camera to turn on grid lines. Those grid lines are marked according to the rule of thirds.

Think of your cover as having that same grid. On page eighty, I've illustrated the grid using two book covers. The four points where the rows and columns intersect are the focal points of the cover. The most important part of your image should touch or be centered on a focal point. The book title should be in either the top row or the bottom row. Or if your title contains a lot of words, try to balance the title above and below the top line. Place the author name below the bottom line so the name is in the bottom third. Adjust any images so the main subject or graphic element is aligned with either the left or right grid line. Do not place the main subject of the image in the center box.

## Book Spine

WHEN YOUR BOOK IS on a shelf, whether in a store or someone's personal library, a person generally sees the spine first. Make sure the spine of your book is eye-catching!

The spine should mimic the front cover design. If possible, use the same font and same coloring for the title. Sometimes due to the size of the spine, it's not possible to mimic the title, especially if a script font was used. In that situation, use a basic font for readability.

The book title should be placed in the top third of the spine. The type runs down the spine and your head should tip to the right when reading the title.

The last name of the author, not the full name, comes after the title and runs in the same direction.

If you have a publishing company logo, place it in the bottom third of the spine. If you don't have a logo, lower the author name to help balance the look on the spine.

The title is in the top row.

The balance of the image is offset, leading the eye downward.

The open book, the main focus of the image, falls in the bottom row and along a vertical line.

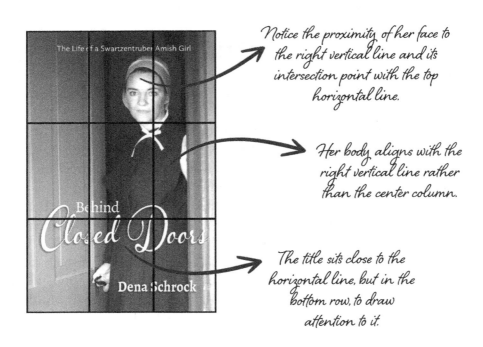

Notice the proximity of her face to the right vertical line and its intersection point with the top horizontal line.

Her body aligns with the right vertical line rather than the center column.

The title sits close to the horizontal line, but in the bottom row, to draw attention to it.

For ideas on how to design your book spine and ways to make the spine stand out, visit a library or bookstore.

## Back Cover

EARLIER, I SAID THAT the front cover is the face of your book. While the back cover may not be as pretty as the front, it is equally important because it's the sales tool for the entire book. The back cover should be attractive, blend with the front cover, and also be readable.

A typical back cover contains the book blurb, author biography, author photo, and ISBN barcode. In chapter five, we talked about the importance of the book blurb. Remember, a blurb should be between 150 and 250 words. If your book is a smaller trim size, aim for a lower word count. The book blurb should shine on the back cover. Use typography and color to draw the reader's eye to the blurb.

The back cover also includes the brief author biography mentioned in chapter four. Limit the biography to a couple of short sentences highlighting your achievements.

The author photo should be crisp and focused. Ideally, a professional headshot is best, but if you can't afford one, have someone take your photo or use selfie mode on your phone. Try to avoid a busy background. Look for a solid color background and wear a color that contrasts with the background. The author photo is typically cropped at the shoulders. If you are creating a brand and your book cover will reflect that brand, make sure your outfit coordinates with your brand colors.

The ISBN barcode is placed in the bottom right corner of the back cover or the bottom middle of the cover. We'll talk more about the ISBN barcode in Chapter Twenty-Four: ISBNs and Barcodes, but for now, know that you do not have to purchase a barcode to use on your back cover.

# 17

# EBOOK DESIGN

EBOOK DESIGN DIFFERS DRAMATICALLY from print design. When a document is designed for print, the creator knows that their design is exactly how the document will look to the reader. For ebooks, the reader controls the look of the page. The reader can choose the font and the font size, and the designer has no control over those choices. Since font choices are up to the reader, page and line breaks are eliminated. A paragraph might have six lines on my screen but have ten lines on your screen because you chose a smaller font size.

Fancy chapter openings and specialty fonts are also out unless they are converted to images and placed at the beginning of the chapter. The downside to using images is that not every reader uses a white background. Popular e-readers have the option for a sepia/cream background and for dark mode. If either is chosen, the fancy chapter-opening image appears with a white box around it.

## What's the difference between reflowable vs. fixed ebooks?

MOST EBOOKS ARE IN reflowable format, which means the document adjusts according to the user's screen. When a reflowable ebook is viewed on a cell phone, lines might include ten words with fifteen lines on the screen. When the same ebook is viewed on a tablet, the ebook reflows, and the reader sees lines with twenty-five words and thirty lines on the screen.

A fixed ebook does not adjust according to the screen. This format is typically used for children's books with pictures and text over the pictures. It's also popular for textbooks and cookbooks, depending on the number of images. The downside to using a fixed format is the reader must zoom in and out or tap the text to read it on a smaller device.

## Do I need to know HTML to create an ebook?

A FEW YEARS AGO, basic HTML knowledge was a necessity to properly create and code an ebook. Now, with the advent of programs like Vellum and Kindle Create, it's much easier to create an ebook based on the visual design versus the hidden HTML coding. However, if you have an ebook with a lot of technical formatting, knowing HTML yourself or hiring someone who does will benefit you.

## What software is available for creating ebooks?

CREATING EBOOKS ISN'T FOR the faint of heart, especially if the ebook will contain images or graphics. The various ebook distributors, such as Draft2Digital, offer options for automatically converting an MS Word document to an ebook. However, by allowing that automatic conversion, you will have zero say in how the ebook looks. If you prefer to create the ebook yourself and maintain some control over the decorative options, I recommend using Vellum, Kindle Create, Atticus, or a similar program. If you are using a Mac, Apple Pages offers export to an ebook, but the customization options are limited.

## Can I use images in an ebook?

YES, YOU CAN USE images in an ebook. The images can be in full color even if the printed version of the book contains grayscale images. If you are using color images, they should be RGB and not CMYK, which is used for color printing. In addition, the image resolution should be reduced according to the ebook distributor's specifications. To find the specifications, search the distributor's help section for ebook formatting guidelines.

## What file type should I use?

IF YOU ARE DISTRIBUTING your ebook via multiple vendors, the best option is an EPUB file. All the major vendors accept EPUBs. Some vendors will convert an MS Word DOCX to the appropriate file type for you, but at that point, you are trusting the vendor that your file will have no mistakes. PDFs are generally not accepted for ebooks.

Amazon KDP used to prefer MOBI files. However, as of August 2021, they changed their guidelines to exclude MOBI for reflowable ebooks. (MOBI is acceptable for fixed-format ebooks.) Reflowable ebooks take the following file types: DOCX, EPUB, and KPF (Kindle Package Format). If Amazon KDP will be your only ebook vendor, you can easily create your ebook using Kindle Create, Amazon's recommended option, to avoid any formatting issues in your ebook. KDP has an informative chart in their help section under "Supported Ebook Formats." The chart gives an overview of each file type, what program to use to create that file type, and what devices the file type is compatible with.

> **TIP**
>
> For a children's picture book, use the Kindle Kids' Book Creator. The tool exports a MOBI file, so you cannot use the file on platforms other than Amason KDP. Download the "KIndle Kids' Book Creator User Guide" for step-by-step directions.

# 18

# FINAL PRINT SUBMISSION FILES

ONCE THE BOOK COVER and interior pages are designed and approved, the next step is uploading and printing. Print facilities accept a variety of file types, but the best type for submission is a Portable Document Format or PDF file.

## Why is a PDF the best?

A PDF LOCKS IN all the formatting and design in a document. The "look" of the document does not change when the PDF is opened on a different computer. Page breaks, line breaks, and font styling stay the same.

Contrast that with an MS Word or Adobe InDesign document where type might reflow when passing the document between a PC and a Mac. The reflowing happens when font files do not match exactly even though the font name is identical.

Because of the unknowns involved when working in a virtual world, PDF format is the best for maintaining control over the look of your printed book.

## Can I submit another file type?

SOME PRINT FACILITIES ALLOW you to submit file types other than a PDF. You can submit those files types, but be aware that the proofs may look different than the file you submitted. Having a book look different than planned is a risk you need to be willing to take. Also, if you used a facility's online book building tool, you will not be able to submit a PDF.

## What type of PDF should I submit?

IF YOU'VE EVER CREATED a PDF, you know that there are multiple options for the PDF presets. Most print facilities request either High Quality Print, Press Quality, or PDF/X-1a:2001.

Pay careful attention to the print facility's PDF requirements. IngramSpark requests PDF/X-1a:2001 PDFs, and Amazon KDP likes Press Quality PDFs. If you submit a Press Quality or High Quality Print to IngramSpark, the file will be accepted, but it will return errors during the validation step. Those errors will probably be related to embedded fonts, image resolution, and image type. Because the PDF/X-1a:2001 is a superior file type to Press Quality, you can submit the PDF/X-1a:2001 to Amazon KDP, and it will be accepted without a problem. If you try to submit a lesser quality PDF, such as a Small File Size, KDP will reject it.

## Do I choose pages or spreads?

WHILE IT'S NICE TO see your book with facing pages laid out in page spreads (two pages side-by-side), most print facilities prefer that PDFs are single pages with one book page showing at a time. The facility will re-assemble the book and create a spread version for the electronic proof. However, some facilities leave the proof version in single pages. Check your print facility's guidelines for specifics about submitting pages or spreads and what format the electronic proof will use.

# How do I embed fonts?

ONE OF THE REQUIREMENTS for submitting final files is that any font used in the document must be embedded. If you or your designer are using the Adobe Creative Cloud suite, fonts are automatically embedded in the PDF as long as the font is a commercial font with the appropriate permissions.

In Microsoft Word, fonts are embedded only if the option for embedding fonts is checked. Go to the File menu. Choose Options. In the box that pops up, choose Save. Under the Save options, check the box to embed fonts.

## How can I check if my fonts are actually embedded?

IF YOU HAVE ADOBE Acrobat Reader, it's simple to check if all fonts are embedded in the PDF. Go to the File menu. Choose Properties. Select the Fonts tab. You should see a list of all the fonts used in your document. If the font is embedded, it will say "Embedded Subset" next to the font name. If for some reason, some of the font family was not embedded, it will say "Partially Embedded Subset." And a font family that is not embedded at all will say "Not Embedded" or something similar.

If the font is not embedded, you have two options. Find a commercial version of the font that can be embedded. Or choose a different font. You cannot force a font to be embedded in a document.

# Part Three

# PRINTING

Do not read this part without reading Part Four: Planning. The decisions you make while planning your book directly affect your printing choices. And your printing choices affect your options while planning.

# 19

# INTRODUCTION TO PRINTING

Books are printed in one of two ways: offset printing and print-on-demand printing (POD). The best printing option for you depends on your book specifications and your ability to invest financially in printing.

When I use the word "offset" in this book, I'm referring to the broad definition of a specialized book printer who offers short or long press runs of a book. The minimum quantity of books for offset printing can be low, sometimes five hundred books or less, and the maximum is in the tens of thousands. I am not distinguishing between print facilities that use digital presses versus offset presses. The distinction is strictly about the ability to do a press run versus POD where a single book is printed when a customer orders it.

## What are the major differences?

The biggest difference between offset printing and POD is the financial investment. Offset requires the author to purchase copies of the book upfront before printing. If production costs for a book are $5.10 and the author wants a thousand copies printed offset, the author will pay the print facility $5,100 plus shipping costs.

With POD, the author pays nothing. The production costs are deducted from the book's retail price paid by the customer. The POD company pays the author their share of book sales every month, and no money leaves the author's pocket for printing. However, the POD company keeps a portion of the sale too, so generally, the author makes less money from a POD sale than from an offset sale. I say "generally" because there are always exceptions, but most of the time, offset gives a better return on the investment.

Another significant difference between offset and POD is the available options for a book. Both models of printing offer color and grayscale. Both offer softcover and hardcover. However, that's where the similarities end. POD is limited by its simplicity. Cover options are basic—matte or gloss finish—compared to offset that allows UV coating, spot varnish, embossed lettering, and so much more. POD also offers basic binding options and is generally a no-go for spiral binding, comb bindings, and thicker lay-flat books. (LuLu, a popular POD company, does offer specialty bindings, but two other popular POD companies, IngramSpark and Amazon KDP, do not.)

Some people cite quality control as a difference as well. With offset printing, the press is set up strictly for your book. Every printed copy of your book will look identical. As the books come off the press, employees check to make sure ink coverage is even and the pages are straight. Later in the process, they check for binding issues and that the trimming is accurate.

With POD, a single copy of your book is printed at a time and follows a variety of other books off of the machine. The POD copy may or may not be flawed, depending on how well the quality control person is paying attention that day. Most books print okay, but the possibility that someone may receive an inferior copy is a risk that comes with POD and one you have to be willing to take in order to skip the offset financial investment.

## How do you choose whether to use offset or POD?

1. If you can't afford to invest from a few hundred to a few thousand dollars upfront, go with POD. It's that simple.

2. You don't have to choose one or the other. You can use both effectively, assuming you are producing an average book. (By "average," I mean a black-and-white book like a paperback or hardcover with no special options.) The recommended route is to use POD companies like IngramSpark for its distribution network and Amazon KDP for its reputation as a book retailer. Then use offset for books you plan to sell in person and via your website.

3. Consider the options you need. POD offers basic options. With offset, the sky is the limit. If you need a specialty binding, like spiral, you'll probably have to use offset. If you are creating a child's board book or a full-color coffee-table photography book, offset is the better—and potentially the only—choice for board books. If you want special options on the cover, you need offset.

## What do I need before printing?

1. The manuscript in its final design. This means the pages look exactly like a book page and not an 8-1/2x11 MS Word document.

2. A complete wraparound cover on the print facility's template. Failure to use the cover template is perhaps the most common problem that causes rejection during the print facility's review stage.

3. Final PDF files. Both the interior pages and the cover of the book should be submitted as two separate PDFs to the print facility. See Chapter Eighteen: Final Print Submission Files for more information about PDF files.

# 20
# BOOK SPECS FOR PRINTING

When you are comparing printing companies, it's important to compare apples to apples for your book specifications or the production details of the book. The type of printing you choose (POD or offset) does not affect your book specs. What is included in the specifications?

## Trim size

Trim size is the dimensions of the book—6x9, 8x10, 5.5x8.5, etc. If you are publishing multiple formats (paperback and hardback), you can use the same trim size for all formats. Using the same size means you can use the same interior page design file and not incur another design fee for a different size.

Not every printer offers every trim size. Verify with your print facility that they offer the size you want. Larger trim sizes, a width of 8.25 and up, can vary between facilities. The book format, hardback versus paperback, and whether the book is color or grayscale also affects the availability of a particular trim size. For example, Amazon KDP offers an 8.25x8.25 color paperback, but IngramSpark does not. However, IngramSpark offers three other large sizes that KDP does not.

# Binding

THE BINDING IS THE format of the book—paperback or hardback. Each format breaks down into additional options:

## Paperback

- **Perfect bound**—Perfect bound is the most popular option, and sometimes the only option, for POD books. The spine is glued together and then the spine is glued to the cover.
- **Saddle stitch**—Saddle stitching uses staples to hold the pages and cover together. It's the recommended binding for children's paperback picture books. Saddle stitching is limited to books with fewer pages, generally under one hundred and possibly less, depending on the print facility.
- **Coil binding**—Popular with workbooks, journals, and cookbooks, coil binding uses a plastic spiral or comb to hold the cover and pages together. No glue is involved.

## Hardback

THE MAJORITY OF HARDBACK books produced via POD use an adhesive just like perfect-bound paperbacks. The pages are glued together, and the casing (the cover) is attached to the pages.

Another popular option not available via POD is Smyth sewn binding. Smyth sewn uses thread to sew together the pages within a signature (eight or sixteen pages) and then sew the signatures to each other. This binding is the most durable binding available for hardback books. Because Smyth sewn does not use glue, the binding lays flat with little page curl toward the center of the book.

Since POD uses the perfect-bound process for hardback books, the specifications for hardbacks break down into the type of cover.

- **Case laminate**—The color cover is printed and glued to the cardboard casing. This style of cover is very similar to a paperback except the cardboard makes the cover stiff and not flexible like a paperback. A dust jacket (the removable paper cover) is optional for a case laminate book.
- **Cloth or linen cover**—A cloth cover is created by printing the book information (title and author name with no images) on a cloth and

adhering the cloth to the casing. The cloth colors are usually dark, and the printing is done in foil ink, such as gold, silver, or blue. Dust jackets are popular with cloth covers because the cloth cover does not contain any images or information about the book.

## Laminate

THE SIMPLEST WAY TO explain laminate is it is the coating that goes on the cover. Most print facilities offer two options: glossy or matte. Glossy creates a shiny cover while matte has a softer sheen to it, making the cover appear almost velvet-like.

Which one is best? It depends on your cover design. Colorful covers or ones with vibrant colors look best in gloss.

## Paper Options

PAPER OPTIONS BREAK DOWN into the color and the weight or thickness of the paper.

Paper color has two basic choices—white or cream. White is popular for non-fiction while cream is popular for fiction. White is recommended for books with grayscale images. Studies have shown that cream is easier on the eyes when reading text-heavy pages. Cream also helps those who struggle with reading disorders, such as dyslexia.

Paper weight can be complicated because you have to compare the weight of the paper plus the type of the paper in order for the comparison to be accurate. I'm not going to go into many details about paper weight, but the one thing you need to know is that the lower the weight number, the thinner the paper.

Paper weight is written in pounds as either 50# or 50 lb. In general, assume that for every ten pounds of weight, the thickness of the paper increases by 10–15%. So 60# paper will be about 10% thicker than 50#, and 70# will be about 20–30% thicker than 50# paper.

Because the individual sheets of paper are thicker, a higher paper weight means an increase in the spine thickness for a book. By carefully selecting paper weight, you can add to the bulkiness of a shorter book or reduce the thickness of a longer book.

If your book contains graphics, charts, or images, consider the paper "bleed through." The lighter the paper, the more chance you have of bleed through happening. Newspapers, which use approximately 30# paper, regularly fall victim to bleed through. Bleed through happens when the words and images from the back side of the page are slightly visible on the front side. Those words and images look almost like shadows. They aren't readable, but you know they are there. To avoid the possibility of bleed through, use a higher paper weight, if available, when you have a lot of images in your book. In general, a text-heavy book that is properly designed will not have problems with bleed through.

## PREMIUM COLOR

POD printers offer standard and premium color. Choose premium for children's books, photography books, and cookbooks. While standard color may seem more cost effective, premium color offers better image clarity and color reproduction.

If you are planning on a color book, definitely choose a high paper weight. Coffee-table photography books often use 100# paper. Children's picture books don't need to be as heavy as a coffee-table book, and 80# is usually sufficient. POD offers a 50# and 70# paper weight for color, and I always recommend the higher weight, especially if the pages will be saturated with ink, e.g., a children's picture book.

Another important paper feature for color printing is whether to use glossy paper or a different finish. The recommendation is to use a matte or satin paper finish if your book has an equal balance of text and color images. If the book is mostly color images with limited text, choose glossy. The gloss will help the image colors pop.

# 21
# PRINT ON
# DEMAND

PRINT-ON-DEMAND (POD) HAS TWO major players—Amazon KDP and IngramSpark.

Amazon revolutionized the publishing industry when it started offering book production options for individuals. A short time later, Ingram Content Group jumped onboard the POD train and created IngramSpark for self-publishing authors. Both companies offer the same binding options, paper options, and cover options. In 2021, KDP added a hardcover option that changed the playing field a bit because, for years, if an author wanted a POD hardcover book, IngramSpark was the only choice.

The major difference between IngramSpark and KDP is the type of company. IngramSpark is a distributor that produces the book and makes it available to thousands of retailers worldwide. IngramSpark itself is not a retailer. You cannot send potential buyers to the Ingram-Spark website to purchase your book. Think of IngramSpark as a behind-the-scenes player.

Amazon KDP, on the other hand, is a retailer. They produce the books and offer them for sale on the Amazon website. KDP offers an

**TIP**

IngramSpark offers Aerio, a retail option that can be integrated into your website and social media. Aerio allows you to sell books directly from Ingram's catalog. Book orders are fulfilled and shipped directly from Ingram.

expanded distribution option that makes a book available to other online retailers. KDP's expanded distribution is not as robust as IngramSpark's even though KDP utilizes IngramSpark's distribution network.

When discussing how to choose between offset and POD printing, I mentioned the possibility of using both IngramSpark and KDP together. This method benefits authors because it plays to the strong points of each company. Ingram has cultivated a huge distribution network of stores, libraries, schools, and online retailers. If you want your book available for purchase just about anywhere, IngramSpark is the answer. However, this increased availability comes with a cost. IngramSpark keeps a small portion of every sale to help support its company.

Before I explain how Ingram keeping a portion of sales affects an author, let's talk about Amazon, the largest book retailer in the world. Most people know that Amazon sells books, so when people are looking for a book, where do they go? To Amazon. The largest portion of your book sales will probably come from Amazon because of its popularity as a book retailer.

If you are considering using IngramSpark, please note that IngramSpark distributes to Amazon. Your book will appear on Amazon, and you won't have to do anything. However, your best option is to set up your book directly with Amazon. When IngramSpark distributes to

Amazon, your compensation amount per sale will be reduced. So for a higher profit, combine IngramSpark and Amazon KDP. Going direct to KDP means you will receive KDP's royalty rate of 60%, which is potentially more than IngramSpark's, depending on your discount settings. However, if you set up your book with both IngramSpark and KDP, an order may be fulfilled using either facility's printer.

# Production Costs

PRODUCTION COSTS INCLUDE THE cost of paper plus the printing and binding of the book. When a sale is made, the production cost is deducted from the sale price and paid to the POD company. The author does not see this money. However, figuring out production costs is an important step in determining a viable retail sales price.

POD production costs are similar between companies. When comparing IngramSpark and Amazon KDP, IngramSpark has higher production costs in general. Every book is different, so consult the Production Cost Calculators available on each company's website.

The calculators will ask for the book specifications—trim size, binding type, paper, page count, grayscale or color, etc. Here's a sample for a paperback book:

> **Specifications:** 5.5x8.5 trim size
> 250 pages
> white paper
> paperback binding
> matte cover

> **IngramSpark cost:** $4.42*

> **Amazon KDP cost:** $3.85

One other note about KDP versus IngramSpark—IngramSpark charges a $49 setup fee for each title and a $25 revision fee. KDP does not have fees. For some, that $49 is a make-or-break deal, but it's a small price to pay to be part of Ingram's large distribution network.

*Cost reflects IngramSpark's pricing as of the November 2021 price increase.

# Other POD Companies

Two other POD companies worth mentioning are LuLu and Draft2Digital. For some authors, these two are viable choices.

Lulu offers some specialty options, such as linen wrap covers and coil binding, which are not offered by KDP and IngramSpark. They also offer distribution via Ingram's network. The downside is that LuLu's cost per book tends to be higher. Using the same book specifications as before, Lulu's cost is $6.90 compared to $3.85 and $4.42.

Draft2Digital, well known for its ebook distribution network, is a newer player in the printed paperback market. Draft2Digital's cost per book is comparable to that of IngramSpark and KDP. Their trim size offerings are not as robust, but they do offer the most popular trim sizes. (At the time of this book's publication, Draft2Digital's paperback program was still in beta. Check their website for updates and availability.)

# 22
# OFFSET PRINTING

WHILE POD FACILITIES PRINT single copies of a book, offset companies print hundreds of copies of a book at a time, which means greater consistency for the physical books. If you know you have the platform or audience to sell hundreds or thousands of books, offset printing is the way to go. You will make more money per book sale as opposed to strictly using POD and ordering author copies.

## How do you find an offset print facility?

YOU CAN FIND AN offset print facility by asking for recommendations from other authors or publishers. There are way too many offset book printing facilities here in North America and overseas to list them all in this book.

Some of the major players I've worked with in the past are Total Printing Solutions, BookMasters (now part of the Baker & Taylor Publisher Services), Sheridan Minnesota (formerly Bang Printing), and 48HourBooks.

A new kid on the block for offset printing is also worth mentioning.

If you don't want to shop around to find an offset printer on your own, the Independent Authors' Publishing Collective (IAPC) might be the solution you need. IAPC finds the best offset deal for your book and does all the legwork for you. They also offer warehousing and distribution options so you don't need to worry about where to store 500 or more books. You can find more information, including a price quote calculator, at iapcbooks.com.

## How is offset pricing different than POD?

HERE'S HOW THE PRICING works for offset—the more copies you order, the cheaper the cost will be per book. If you place a bulk order via a POD company, the cost per book stays the same. For example, one book costs $4.42, 100 books cost $442.00, and 1,000 books cost $4,420.00. There is zero difference in the cost per book. With offset pricing, the larger the quantity, the cheaper the total cost. (See the following section for a specific example.)

## What about production costs?

THE PRODUCTION COSTS FOR offset printing include the same options as POD—paper, printing, and binding. Most offset book printing companies have an instant quote calculator on their website. The calculator makes it easy to compare pricing for different companies. Some calculators only allow the basics with no specialty options; others include the specialty choices. Once you've narrowed down your options to a couple of companies, request a full quote from each one to guarantee the calculator was accurate for your book specifications.

Using the same paperback specifications as the example for POD production costs in the previous chapter, here's a cost example from Sheridan Minnesota:

**100 books:** $5.45 per book or $545.00 upfront
**1,000 books:** $2.34 per book or $2,340 upfront
**10,000 books:** $1.84 per book or $18,400 upfront

Note the significant cost savings as the quantity increases. Also note that an order of 1,000 books would save $1.51 per book over KDP's cost.

Using the same specifications, here are the costs from 48HourBooks:

**100 books:** $5.04 per book or $504 upfront
**1,000 books:** $4.33 per book or $4,330 upfront
**10,000 books:** $3.82 per book or $38,200 upfront

48HourBooks guarantees books will ship within forty-eight hours of the author approving the proof. Because of this guarantee, their cost per book isn't significantly different than POD. However, the turn-around time is considerably better. When I started writing this book, POD was a minimum ten-day wait from the time of order placement until the shipping of books. Less than two months later, that window expanded to twenty-one days. POD turnaround time is regulated by demand, so if you choose a busy time of the year to launch your book or place an order, you might have a longer wait than expected.

Based on the price comparison between Sheridan Minnesota and 48HourBooks, Sheridan Minnesota would be the better option for the larger quantities. If you are in a rush to receive your books, 48Hour-Books is the faster option.

# Case Study #2

JOHN, A WELL-KNOWN SPEAKER in religious circles, was faced with the dilemma of how much to invest in printing his books. He had speaking engagements already on his calendar, and he knew he could sell a significant quantity of books. He planned on starting with a hardcover and adding a paperback later.

He shopped around for pricing and even considered bulk ordering author copies from IngramSpark as needed. However, the cost per book from IngramSpark was $9.32. He checked on offset printing and found a price of $2.20 per book for 15,000 books. That meant he'd have to pay $33,000 upfront to order his books. That $33,000 is a large sum of money to part with, but I encouraged John to consider what the numbers meant in the long run.

Ordering 15,000 books as needed from IngramSpark would cost him $139,800 over time. One offset bulk order of 15,000 copies would cost a onetime payment of $33,000.

John planned to set his retail price at $25.99 for his hardcover book. To determine his gross profit per book for direct sales, subtract the production cost per book from the retail price.

**IngramSpark:** $25.99 − $9.32 = $16.67 profit per book sold.
**Offset:** $25.99 − $2.20 = $23.79 profit per book sold.

**Total gross profit\* selling 10,000 books:**
IngramSpark—$250,050
Offset—$356,850.

**That's an income difference of $106,800.**

\*His net profit would be less after deducting his editing, design, marketing, and miscellaneous costs.

When John decided to invest the $33,000 in printing, he didn't have the full amount available. He understood the risk and reward of investing in his book, so he borrowed a portion of the money from a family member. He wrote up a contract, including a repayment schedule, and they both signed the contract in front of a notary. He also did pre-orders with special incentives via his website. In the end, he was happy with his decision and has gone on to produce other books using offset printing.

Part Four

# PLANNING

# 23
# INTRODUCTION TO PLANNING

WHILE YOUR BOOK IS in the editing and design phases, you should be preparing for the production stage of your book. The first step is to establish your publishing company name. Next, set up your accounts at whichever print facilities you plan to use. (See Part Four: Printing for more information about choosing a print facility.) You will also need an International Standard Book Number (ISBN) and a barcode if you are creating a print book. (Ebooks do not need a barcode, and depending on your choice of ebook distributor, you may not need an ISBN.) Some authors choose to register with the Library of Congress and the US Copyright office as well.

## Publishing Company

WHEN YOU CREATE VARIOUS accounts at the different vendors, they will ask for your publishing company name. If you intend to publish multiple books, you should establish a formal publisher name rather than using your personal name. While using your name is acceptable, a company name shows potential readers that you are serious about publishing.

Companies like Amazon and IngramSpark can issue royalties under your name or your publishing company name. If you register your publishing company with your state's secretary of state as a formal business (whether an LLC, a doing-business-as, a sole proprietor, or some other business entity), you can establish financial accounts for royalties and sales under the business name. Please consult an accountant and an attorney for which business scenario would be best in your situation.

## Imprints

WHEN YOU ASSIGN AN ISBN to a book or upload to a POD company, you'll see an option labeled "Imprint." The imprint name is the name you want to appear as the "Publisher" in the online listings for the book. The imprint name is different than the publishing company name.

A publishing company acts as the umbrella company and can be divided into imprints or mini-companies. Each imprint publishes a specific type of book. Most large, established traditional publishers use imprints to represent their different arms of publishing. For example, Penguin Random House has 275 different imprint names. Popular imprints you might recognize are Penguin Books, Penguin Classics, Ballantine Books, Bantam, and Rodale.

Under what circumstances is an imprint name a good idea for a self-publishing author? Consider Janice. She has established herself as a contemporary steamy romance author with six-figure sales. But her kids begged her to write stories for them, so she decided to try writing middle-grade fiction. She plans to write under a pseudonym or pen name so the middle-grade fiction isn't associated with her steamy romances. She uses her same publishing company to publish the books but creates a separate imprint for her middle-grade fiction because she wants to disassociate her two author personas.

An imprint can be your name or anything you choose. If you aren't going to use your name, I recommend trying to find an imprint that doesn't already exist. Use Google and the search tool on Amazon to test possibilities. While there are no regulations for imprint names, avoid using those associated with the big publishers.

# 24

# ISBNS AND BARCODES

EVERY PRINTED BOOK OFFERED for sale is required to have an International Standard Book Number or ISBN, which is the numerical identification code for the book. No two ISBNs are the same. The ISBN identifies the country of origin, the book language, the publisher, and the individual title.

Each country has an established ISBN agency that provides the numbers to authors. (Check your country at isbn-international.org /agencies.) Do not purchase an ISBN from anywhere but the agency for your country. Some countries offer a limited number of ISBNs for free to authors, while other countries, like the US, require authors to purchase their ISBNs. It's important to check with the ISBN agency in your country so you know the specific regulations for your country.

ISBNs do not expire. Once you purchase one, it is yours to use whenever you want.

## Who is required to have an ISBN?

IF A BOOK IS placed for sale on a retailer's website, an ISBN is required.

Each format—paperback, hardback, ebook, audiobook—requires its own ISBN. The same book published as a paperback and a hardback means the author needs two ISBNs.

Ebooks are not required to have an ISBN unless the book will be distributed via a distribution service like IngramSpark, Draft2-Digital, or Smashwords. These services offer free ISBNs, but just like free ISBNs for print books, the free ISBN is limited to only that distribution service. If you plan to upload directly to multiple retailers (KDP, Kobo, Google Play, Apple iBooks, and Barnes and Noble), purchase an ISBN for your ebook.

## Where can I purchase an ISBN?

IN THE US, THE official agency for ISBNs is Bowker. The website for Bowker (bowker.com) has loads of resources for authors. However, to purchase an ISBN, go to Bowker's sister site—myidentifiers.com.

## Should I purchase in bulk?

WHEN PURCHASING ISBNs, CONSIDER your end game with publishing. Will you write more than one book? Will you publish your book in more than one format? If so, you may want to purchase a package of ISBNs from Bowker. They offer packages of 10, 100, and 1,000 for authors. (Publishing companies can purchase larger quantities.) Let's look at the math.

> 1 ISBN from Bowker = $125
> 10 ISBNs = $295
> 100 ISBNs = $575
> 1000 ISBNs = $1,500

As you can see, the more ISBNs you purchase, the cheaper the individual ISBN is. Very few authors will need 1,000 ISBNs, but the 10 or 100 may be a viable option for those writing series and publishing in multiple formats.

# Should I buy a discounted ISBN from IngramSpark?

EARLIER I SAID TO not purchase an ISBN from anywhere but the agency in your country. The exception to that statement is the discounted ISBN offered via IngramSpark. Bowker and IngramSpark established a partnership to offer discounted ISBNs to authors who need single ISBNs.

During the title setup process on the IngramSpark website, you will see three options:

- Provide your own ISBN,
- Purchase a Bowker ISBN (discounted to $85), and
- Use a free ISBN.

If you plan to publish only one book in one or two formats, purchasing the discounted ISBN is a better option than going directly to Bowker where a single ISBN costs $125. We can see that $85 is cheaper than $125.

IngramSpark's discounted ISBN is identical to purchasing an ISBN from Bowker. It does not have any limitations, and you can use the ISBN at other print facilities. When you purchase the discounted ISBN, you will be redirected to the Bowker website to register and assign the ISBN.

# Should I use a free ISBN?

YOU MIGHT HAVE HEARD that sites like Amazon KDP and Ingram-Spark offer free ISBNs to authors. Free sure is better than paying $125 for a single ISBN, right? Not necessarily. It depends on your publishing model. A purchased ISBN allows you to publish and sell your books wherever you want. You can upload to multiple print facilities and distributors using the same ISBN with zero limitations.

A free ISBN comes with limitations. The biggest one is the ISBN is valid only on the site providing the free ISBN. If you plan to publish on only one site, such as KDP, and use only that site's distribution options, the free ISBN is acceptable. KDP and IngramSpark both list the free ISBN limitations on their websites, and I encourage you to read the list before deciding to use a free ISBN.

Another big difference between a purchased and a free ISBN is the publisher name. Unlike a purchased ISBN, a free ISBN lists the publisher name as "independently published." There's no option to change the name either. For some, the "independently published" name doesn't matter because they only intend to sell via one retailer, but for those who plan to market to bookstores or libraries, the name can act as a red flag to potential retail buyers. Sadly, not everyone who self-publishes adheres to professional standards, and quite frankly, some horrible books out there give the self-publishing industry a bad name. A bookstore or retail store might refuse to order or carry a book if they see the "independently published" name.

If you plan to use IngramSpark and KDP together, you should purchase your ISBN. You could use a free ISBN from each site, but because IngramSpark distributes to KDP, using two free ISBNs creates two listings of your book on KDP.

Please exercise caution when deciding whether to use a free ISBN. Once you publish a book with an ISBN, you cannot change the ISBN later on without unpublishing the book and potentially losing reviews and rankings.

## How do I assign an ISBN?

ONCE YOU HAVE PURCHASED an ISBN, you need to assign the ISBN to the book. You can assign the ISBN at any point in the process, but you should probably wait until your front cover is finalized and you've nailed down the specifics of pricing and a release date.

To assign an ISBN, go to the myidentifiers.com website and log in to your account. Under the My Identifiers tab, you will see a list of the ISBNs you purchased. Click on "Assign" next to the ISBN you want to use. Next, fill in the specifics about the title. The fields marked with a red asterisk are required. Others are optional but recommended.

Title information—Input your book title.

Medium and Format—Select whether the book's format is print, electronic, or audio.

Subject and Genre—The list contains broad topics. Choose the closest fit to your book's genre.

Author and Contributor—Enter your author information. If you want to recognize other contributors, such as an illustrator, add another contributor and enter the information.

Sales and Pricing:

**TIP**

In the upper righthand corner of the form is the option to choose between the "Short" or "Expanded" form. The Expanded form asks for additional details about the title. The Expanded form is recommended if you are publishing a multi-volume work, a different edition, or a book in another language.

- Publisher—If you need to publish under an imprint name, make sure you choose the imprint from the "Publisher" list. (You can create an imprint under "My Profile Data" at the top of the screen. After creating the imprint, return to the publisher list and choose the imprint.)

- Publication date—The date you expect the book to be available for purchase.

- Title status—Most books are "Active Record." If your book becomes unavailable in the future, update this section to "Out of Print."

- Target audience—Unless a book specifically fits in one of the other categories, choose "Trade."

- Pricing—Enter your retail price. You can update the title later if you change the pricing.

Cover image—Upload a front cover image. Some retailers will pull the image from the Bowker listing rather than from the distributor, so make sure you add a current cover image.

# Do I need a barcode?

EVERY BOOK SOLD IN a retail setting—whether online or in a brick-and-mortar store—is required to have a barcode on the back cover. The barcode includes the ISBN identifying the book and the retail price (optional). A barcode is unique to an individual book and cannot be used for a different book. If you are publishing both a paperback and a hardcover book, you need two different barcodes because each format requires a different ISBN.

# Do I purchase a barcode?

WHEN YOU PURCHASE AN ISBN, you might see an offer to purchase a barcode. Buying a barcode is not a necessity and is not recommended. Websites like bookow.com generate free barcodes for books. Ingram-Spark provides a free barcode on its cover template, and KDP automatically places a barcode on any cover that does not already have one. If you use IngramSpark's cover template generator, you can copy and paste that barcode to any other cover templates for the same format of the book.

Do not copy a barcode for a paperback book to the template for a hardback book and vice versa. Remember, one book format equals one barcode, just like an ISBN.

# Should the retail price be included in the barcode?

INCLUDING THE PRICE IS not necessary, but it does help retailers. If your book is entering the distribution network and you are planning to market to physical stores, you should embed your retail price in the barcode. Some retailers require the embedded price before physically stocking the book. When deciding whether to include the price, research local stores that are part of your marketing plan. If you plan to do book signings, find out the price requirement for the store so they will stock your book before the signing.

For example, all books stocked in a Barnes & Noble store must have the price embedded in the barcode and include the price in a readable format (US: $9.99) above the barcode. In addition to the price requirements, Barnes & Noble also requires the allowing of returns and a 53%–55% wholesale discount before they will consider stocking a book in a physical store. If your book does not meet these requirements, you will probably be turned down.

## What happens if I change my retail price?

IF YOU DO NOT have the price embedded in your barcode, you do not need to make any changes to your actual book files. Just change the price on your print facility dashboard. However, with an embedded price in the barcode, changing your retail price means updating your cover file. You will need a new barcode with the new price embedded in it. Replace the old barcode with the new barcode and upload your revised files to your print facility. If you are using IngramSpark, updating the cover file means incurring a $25 revision fee. You will pay that fee every time you change your price and update your cover, so make sure you are strategic about your price changes.

# 25
# LIBRARY OF CONGRESS

THE LIBRARY OF CONGRESS (loc.gov) offers two programs to help libraries catalog books. The first program, Cataloging in Publication (CIP), is only available to publishers, not self-publishers. The CIP data creates a bibliographic record for the book that is printed on the book's copyright page and also disseminated to libraries. The CIP is equivalent to the library card catalog information for a book.

The second program is the Preassigned Control Number (PCN) that assigns Library of Congress Control Numbers (LCCN). This program is available to self-publishers; however, the program also has limitations as to what types of materials can receive a number. For example, a title has to appear in print in order for an LCCN to be assigned. Ebooks are not eligible.

Participating in these programs is not a necessity, but if you plan to market to libraries, an LCCN is recommended.

Go to loc.gov/publish/pcn/about/process.html to learn more about the LCCN and follow the PrePub Book Link to register and receive an assigned LCCN. Once you receive the LCCN, place it on the copyright page like this—

Library of Congress Control Number: xxxxxxxxxx

During the registration process, they will ask how many pages are in the book. These are not manuscript pages but the number of book pages after the book is properly designed. Because the number of pages is a necessity, you cannot apply for an LCCN until you have an approximation of your final page count. Once you apply, it takes anywhere from twenty-four hours to two weeks to receive an LCCN.

# 26
# COPYRIGHT

Under US law, your book is copyrighted the minute that you create and begin writing it whether on paper or in an electronic format. You do not need to formally register your book with the government to be protected by copyright laws. However, books that are formally registered have more protections and legal options available if a question arises about infringement (someone using your work without permission).

A copyright myth: Some people suggest mailing a printed copy of your manuscript to yourself as proof of copyright. According to the US Copyright Office website, this method does not give any more protection than the regular copyright that exists the minute you start writing. The only way to formally protect your work is to register it with the Copyright Office.

If you have questions about copyright beyond what is included below, please visit copyright.gov/help/faq/index.html. The website has numerous documents available that explain copyright in detail.

## When do you register your copyright?

You can register before or after publication. For ebooks, you can register any time. For print, if you register before publication, you can submit an electronic copy of your book. Registering after publication requires mailing a printed copy of the "best edition" of the book to the Library of Congress Copyright Office. "Best edition" is determined by the book format and binding. If you publish both hardback and paperback, the hardback is considered the best edition. You can read more about "best edition" at copyright.gov/circs/circ07b.pdf.

Electronic registrations are processed anywhere from one to eight months after submission. Mail-in registrations take longer, possibly up to two years. Remember, your work is copyrighted the minute that you put it on paper, so you are still protected even while waiting for the formal paperwork from the Copyright Office.

Investment: Depending on your situation, a single copyright can cost $45–$65. Other situations can cost up to $200.

## How do I register?

To REGISTER YOUR WORK, go to copyright.gov/registration and click the "Log in to eCO" button. You will be sent to a registration page to create a username and password.

To complete the copyright process, you will need the following information:

- Type of work—Copyright applies to more than books, so you will need to choose "Literary Work" from the menu.

- Title—This is your book title.

- Previous publication—Assuming you haven't published the work before, choose "no" and enter the expected year of publication.

- Author—Enter your author name. If you use a pseudonym (pen name) or want to remain anonymous, check the appropriate box. Whatever name you use on this page will be public record and available online.

- Contact info—Fill in the details as to how you want the Copyright Office to contact you. They will mail your copyright certificate to the address you list, so make sure the address will remain valid for the next six months or longer in case your application is delayed.

Once you process all the above information, the application asks additional questions. Read through each page and proceed according to your individual situation. When the application is complete, you will be required to pay the fee and then submit your work.

If you have previously published books that you have not registered for copyright, the registration process has an option for registering those.

# 27
# PRINT FACILITY ACCOUNTS

SETTING UP AN ACCOUNT with a print facility is straightforward. They ask for contact and financial information.

In situations where the facility will be paying you royalties, such as IngramSpark or Amazon KDP, you need to provide your taxpayer identification number and details for the financial account where you want your royalties deposited. Asking for this information is not a scam. The facility needs your bank account information in order to pay you the royalties. If you are worried about sharing your bank information online, consider setting up a bank account strictly for royalty payments or using a service like PayPal to receive your payments. Do not be skeptical when a facility asks for personal information as part of the process. They are required by the US government to report royalties paid to authors, so they need your personal information.

## What is my Taxpayer Identification Number (TIN)?

IN MOST CASES, THE TIN is either your social security number (SSN) or your employer identification number (EIN). Not everyone has an EIN, but if you are wary of sharing your SSN online, I recommend researching whether an EIN would be appropriate in your situation. You can learn more about EINs at irs.gov/businesses/small-businesses-self-employed/employer-id-numbers.

## Do I need to sign Forms or Agreements?

AFTER YOU INPUT THE required information to set up your account, you may need to electronically sign some forms and agree to the Terms and Conditions for using the print facility. The agreements at the end of the IngramSpark account setup include an agreement for Amazon KDP and Apple iBooks. If IngramSpark is distributing your ebook (not print book), please review these agreements carefully and make whichever choice best fits your situation.

Once you complete the registration process, you can start the Title Setup process and upload your book.

# 28
# TITLE SETUP

THE UPLOADING PROCESS FOR a print facility that is not a retailer or distributor is simple. The website will ask for the book specifications and your payment and then verify your uploaded files. Once those steps are complete, your book enters the facility's system. You will receive a digital proof to review within twenty-four to forty-eight hours, although it may take longer during busy times. After you approve the proof, your books are printed and shipped.

If you are uploading to a retailer or distributor, the process is a little more complicated because you must enter all the details about the book. The following section will walk you through each step and briefly explain best practices for the steps.

Since it is impossible to cover the details about every possible print situation out there in this book, I recommend utilizing the FAQ and resources offered by your print facility.

Amazon KDP—kdp.amazon.com/en_US/help
Draft2Digital—draft2digital.com/faq
IngramSpark—help.ingramspark.com
Lulu—help.lulu.com

## Step One: Ebook or Print

WHEN YOU START A new title setup, the first question is what type of book you are uploading. The answer here determines the questions that follow. IngramSpark allows you to select Print Only, Ebook Only, or Print and Ebook. Amazon KDP offers Ebook, Paperback, or Hardcover. Also, IngramSpark asks if you will be uploading files or using their book building tool. Because the print process requires more details, some of the following steps will be specific to a print book.

## Step Two: Title Information

THE TITLE INFORMATION SECTION is all the details about the book. This information is what appears in the book's online listings. You must input and review these details carefully. If you are uploading to multiple online sites, the information must match exactly to prevent duplicate listings. You will need the following information in no specific order.

**Book title**—Make sure this matches the title on your cover and for your assigned ISBN.

**Subtitle**—If you don't have a subtitle, skip this section.

**Series or Edition**—Enter this information if necessary.

## TIP

When uploading to multiple sites, create a new MS Word document and copy/paste all the pieces of information listed into the document. Then copy/paste from the document to the various sites. This guarantees that your book details will match.

**Author**—Input the author name how it appears on the cover. Using a pseudonym (pen name) is permitted. If the book has more than one author, this should be the primary author's name. Additional authors are added as contributors.

IngramSpark allows you to add additional details about the author, including a biography, prior work, and affiliations. This information is not necessary for a title but can help with search engine optimization for the book.

**Contributors**—Acknowledge an illustrator, photographer, editor, and others in this section. Please confirm with the individual that it is okay to list their name.

**Description**—This is the sales copy that appears with your book title. You can use the blurb from the back of the book, or you can make the description longer.

IngramSpark also has a Short Description. It is not required, but the information is used in their catalogs and by some online retailers.

**Categories**—The categories are based on BISAC codes (bisg.org /page/BISACSubjectCodes). The category determines where a book is placed on a shelf in a physical store or where it is found in an online search. Try to avoid the General categories and be as specific as possible for your genre. For example, a non-fiction book about retirement planning could be classified under Business & Economics/Personal Finance/General, but there's a specific category for retirement planning, so the book should go in Business & Economics/Personal Finance/Retirement Planning.

## CATEGORIES

If you need help with categories and keywords for your book, look at the competition. Study the online listings of other books in your genre. Two sites offering insight into categories are:

Publisher Rocket
publisherrocket.com

Catfinder at
Universal Book Links
bklnk.com/categories5.php

The goal is to place your book in the best category for the content, however, sometimes a specific category doesn't exist. For example, a historical fiction book set during the early 1860s should be placed in Fiction/Historical/Civil War Era. But if the book is a historical romance, the romance categories are based on broader time periods (Medieval, Regency, Renaissance, etc.), so the best match for the early 1860s historical romance would be Fiction/Romance /Historical/American.

Amazon uses the two categories that you choose plus your keywords to determine additional Browse Categories. Amazon thinks potential buyers might choose these categories to find your book. For more information about updating your categories, visit kdp .amazon.com/en_US/help/topic/G200652170.

**Keywords**—These are the words you think someone may use in a search to find your book. Amazon limits keywords to seven total. (You can add more keywords later via Amazon's Author Central.) Ingram-Spark recommends *at least* seven keywords, but not more than 500 total characters.

**Other information**—You will need to choose the book audience (children, young adult, academic, adult, etc.), the imprint name, and whether you own the publishing rights. IngramSpark offers additional optimization information for each title. You can utilize these fields if you want, but they are not required.

## Step Three: Print Information

THIS SECTION COVERS THE production details for your book. This is where you choose your book specifications from Chapter Twenty: Book Specifications for Printing.

**Trim size**—This is the final dimensions of the printed book. Popular dimensions are 5.25x8, 5.5x8.5, and 6x9. Different facilities offer different dimensions, so make sure the trim size you choose is available and that your files match the trim size exactly.

**Color or Black and White**—Your answer here determines paper choices and the production cost for your book. Color printing costs considerably more than black and white. Do not choose color if you do not have color in the book. For POD, one color page means the entire book is considered color.

**Paper**—Choose the color of the paper and the paper weight. Remember, white is recommended if you have images or graphics. A higher paper weight means thicker paper. Some facilities charge extra for higher weights.

**Binding**—If different bindings are available for the book format (paperback, hardback, etc.), that choice is offered here.

**Laminate Type**—Decide if you want gloss or matte finish for the cover.

**Page Count**—The specifications entered plus the page count will determine the production cost for the book. The page count includes every page of the book, including blank pages. The final page count total should be an even number.

Because book signatures are typically printed in multiples of 4, 8, or 16, a print facility may add blank pages to the back of your book. (Ingram-Spark requires the last page of the book to be blank because they place their print information on that page.) To avoid having the print facility add multiple blank pages to the back of your book, make sure your total page count is divisible by 4 minus 1. For example, 260 pages divided by 4 = 65. If you submit a 260-page PDF file, the print facility will probably add four blank pages to the back of your book. To avoid having those pages added, reduce the overall page count by one. So instead of 260 pages, adjust the book design so you have 259 pages or submit a 260-page PDF with the last page blank.

**TIP**

Amazon KDP asks about "Bleed" or "No Bleed" on the print information screen. Choose Bleed only if you have images or graphics that extend to the very edge of the page. The average fiction book does not use bleed. Children's picture books often use bleed.

**Publication Date**—This is the date that your book will go on sale and be available for buyers (individuals and retailers) to purchase.

If you want to set up pre-orders for print or ebook, you need to set the Publication Date and On Sale Date to a future date and then enable distribution. Unfortunately, pre-orders can be persnickety to set up. Amazon KDP allows pre-orders for ebooks, but not print books. Before opting to do a pre-order with IngramSpark, read this article—help.ingramspark.com/hc/en-us/articles/360027788051-On-Sale-Date.

# 29
# PRICING, DISCOUNTS & RETURNS

AFTER ENTERING THE SPECIFICATIONS for the book, you will see the cost to produce your book. The next step is to determine your retail price, what wholesale discount you will offer retailers, and if you will accept returns. The options you choose in this step determine the royalty you make per book sale. Note: For the sake of simplicity, I use the term *royalty* to mean any compensation you receive for book sales from any vendor or distributor.

If you are selling a print book on your own and not through an online retailer,

**Royalty = retail price – production cost.**

If you are selling a book through a distributor like IngramSpark,

**Royalty = (retail price – wholesale discount) – production cost.**

For direct sales through Amazon KDP,

**Royalty = 60% of retail price – production cost.**

Ebook royalties are calculated differently. Ebooks do not have production costs, so companies typically offer a flat rate royalty. Draft-2Digital offers a royalty of roughly 60% of the retail price. Amazon KDP is a bit more complicated. They offer a 70% royalty and a 35% royalty. Most ebooks qualify for the 70% royalty. You can read more about the 70% versus 35% royalty here: kdp.amazon.com/en_US/help/topic/G200634500.

## How should I price my print book?

SOME PEOPLE RANDOMLY ASSIGN a retail price. But rather than shooting in the dark and hoping you hit the target, use some strategy.

1. Formula
   I SAW THIS FORMULA shared in a Facebook group, and I liked how it gives a starting point for pricing. If you know where this formula originated, please let me know so I can give credit where it is due.

   **(Word count / 250) x .06 = minimum retail price**

   Once you know the production costs for your book, start with this retail price and calculate the royalty using the formulas at the beginning of this chapter.

2. Research
   GO TO A BRICK-AND-MORTAR bookstore or browse online for books in your genre. For each book, write down the price and the page count. (Online listings include the page count in the publication details about the book.)
   Once you note the information for about ten books, look for a pattern. What's the highest retail price? Lowest retail price? How about the average or most common price? Is your page count close to any of the books?
   Typically, higher page count books will have a higher retail price because more pages equal a higher production cost.
   Be careful to not compare the pricing of your book with books outside your genre. Pricing can be genre-specific, so make sure you compare apples to apples. A 45,000-word memoir can sell all day

long at $18.99, but a 45,000-word romance novel will struggle at that price.

Do the numbers from the formula and your research line up? Chances are the formula price is at the lower end of, or possibly below, the range you found during research. If that's the case, go with the retail price from the research.

Once you settle on a possible retail price, enter it on the online retailer's site to see what your royalty will be. Remember, the retailer's site is giving you the royalty for books sold through them only. Each retailer will differ slightly. Your retail price should be the same across all retailers, so check each site. Once you have an acceptable royalty amount, move on.

## What is the Wholesale Discount for distribution?

THE WHOLESALE DISCOUNT APPLIES if your book is entering distribution. If you are selling strictly through Amazon KDP's expanded distribution, you do not need to worry about setting a wholesale discount.

The wholesale discount determines the price that a retailer will pay to purchase your book. For any product that a retailer sells, they have to make a profit. That profit allows them to make money and keep their business going. So the retailer looks for deals that will give them the best profit. In the book world, retailers look for a significant discount off the retail price.

Amazon KDP's Expanded Distribution offers a standard 40% discount to retailers. This discount cannot be changed. IngramSpark allows you, the author, to set the discount anywhere between 30% and 55% off retail. Here are three important things to understand about wholesale discounts:

1. The larger the wholesale discount, the less royalty you will make per sale.

2. As previously mentioned, brick-and-mortar stores prefer a 53%–55% discount via IngramSpark.

3. IngramSpark keeps roughly 15% of the wholesale discount to help

recoup costs for maintaining its distribution network. While you see the 55% discount on your dashboard, the retailer sees a 40% wholesale discount when placing an order.

The general recommendation among indie authors is to use the 55% discount only if you will be aggressively marketing to brick-and-mortar stores. Otherwise, choose a lesser discount. The lesser discount puts more money in your pocket versus the retailers' pockets.

## How does the wholesale discount work?

LET'S SAY MATTHEW WROTE a short self-help book. His production cost is $2.30 per book. He's considering whether to set his retail price at $7.99 or $9.99. To figure out his royalties with the different discounts, use these formulas:

**Retail price x discount = wholesale discount cost, then**
**(Retail price - wholesale discount cost) - production cost = royalty.**

Here's the math if Matthew offers a 55% discount.
$9.99 × .55 = $5.49, then
($9.99 – $5.49) – $2.30 = $2.20 royalty.

A 40% discount looks like this:
$9.99 × .4 = $3.99, then
($9.99 – $3.99) – $2.30 = $3.70 royalty.

And a 30% discount looks like this:
$9.99 × .30 = $2.99, then
(9.99 – $2.99) – $2.30 = $4.70 royalty.

Now, here's the same math but using the $7.99 retail price:
For 55%,
$7.99 × .55 = $4.39, then
($7.99 – $4.39) – $2.30 = $1.30.

For 40%,
$7.99 × .4 = $3.20, then
($7.99 – $3.20) – $2.30 = $2.49.

For 30%,

$$\$7.99 \times .35 = \$2.39, \text{ then}$$
$$(\$7.99 - \$2.80) - \$2.30 = \$3.30.$$

Both retail prices give Matthew a decent profit at any wholesale discount level. He likes the numbers he sees, so he decides to launch the book with a $9.99 retail price. He figures that over time his sales numbers might dwindle and he can always offer a price of $7.99 or slightly lower if he wants to run a special. Remember, it's always best to start high with your price and go lower later, rather than start low and try to raise your price.

If Matthew isn't going to market his book to brick-and-mortar stores, he can choose the 30% discount for $9.99 and pocket that additional $2 or more per book sold. Once his book picks up traction and stores express interest, Matthew can log in to his dashboard and change the wholesale discount at any time.

After calculating your royalties with the discounts, ask yourself whether the royalty amounts are acceptable. How many books will you need to sell at each discount level in order to recoup your costs? What if you raised your retail price by one dollar? Does that one dollar keep your retail price within the range for your genre? Now, how many will you need to sell? And what wholesale discount makes the most sense for your situation?

## What are Returns?

How SHOULD YOU HANDLE returns? This is a murky area with no right or wrong choice. The decision to allow or not allow returns comes down to the risk the individual author is willing to take. If you are using only Amazon KDP, you do not have to worry about setting a return status. However, for those distributing via IngramSpark, you need to make a choice.

Remember, like any of the other pricing options, the choice you initially make during title setup is not locked in, and you can log in to your dashboard at any time and make changes. However, when you change the return status, the change may not go into effect immediately. Depending on the change, retailers are permitted to return titles for up to six months after a return status changes. If you are considering allow-ing returns, please read this helpful article— help.ingramspark.com/hc/en-us/articles/209072526-Returns-Information.

## What do the options mean?

RETURNS OFFERS THREE OPTIONS:

- No
- Yes—Deliver
- Yes—Destroy

Bookstores prefer to see a return option because they want to pro-tect their monetary investment in your book. Let's say Smith's Book-store agrees to order ten copies of Matthew's book. Smith's isn't going to pay the full retail price of $9.99 for ten copies because the store needs to make some sort of profit. Since Matthew set his wholesale discount to 55%, the store pays $6 per copy plus shipping and plans to sell the book at the $9.99 retail price. After six months, Smith's sold only three of the ten copies ordered, so they decide to pull the book from their shelves. Matthew's return option determines what happens next.

If Matthew chose "No" and will not accept returns, the bookstore takes a loss. They will probably place the book on sale and hope it moves the copies. Depending on the sale price, the store might recoup the remainder of the $60 investment or they might not. However, this scenario probably won't happen because bookstores will rarely stock a book that does not have a return option. They will special order a title if a customer requests it, but they will not stock the book on their shelves.

If Matthew chose either of the "Yes" options, the bookstore pack-ages the books and sends them back to IngramSpark. Does the store lose its investment in the books? No, IngramSpark refunds their money for the returned books. Good deal, right? For Smith's Bookstore, yes. For Matthew, not so much.

Any returned books plus a shipping cost are charged to the author's account. Depending on the number of books returned, an author's return bill could climb high quickly. Let's consider the math.

Smith's Bookstore purchased ten copies of Matthew's book at $6 per book. Matthew had his retail discount set to 55%, so he made $2.20

per copy sold. Smith's sold three copies, and Matthew received $6.60 in royalties ($2.20 x 3 = $6.60). Now, Smith's returned the remaining seven books. Matthew receives a bill for $42 plus shipping costs ($6 x 7 = $42). Instead of making money, Matthew has now lost a significant amount of money.

## What's the difference between "Return and Destroy" and "Return and Deliver"?

RETURN AND DESTROY MEANS the books are returned to the distributor and destroyed. Those copies are not offered for sale again. Return and Deliver means that the books are eventually returned to the author with the author consuming a $2 per book shipping cost.

There's no guarantee that returned books are suitable for resale. Some authors get lucky and receive copies in decent condition. Others, not so much. Remember, these books have sat in a retail store for an extended period of time. The covers could be bent or torn; inside pages may have marks and stains from buyers browsing through the book.

When it comes to returns, carefully consider your risks. If you are actively marketing your book and you have the financial means to pay for returns, the choice to accept returns may boost your sales. Remember, brick-and-mortar stores love returns. If you do not have the financial means to pay for returns, don't accept them. I've heard scary stories of authors receiving hefty bills in excess of $1,000 for returns. I've also heard stories of authors never receiving a bill. You need to decide if you can take that risk and if that risk aligns with your marketing plan.

# 30
# UPLOADING
# FILES

Uploading book files is as simple as clicking the appropriate button, choosing the file from your computer, hitting upload, and waiting for your file to upload and be validated.

Unfortunately, indie authors have the most problems with the validation process. If your book files are not created correctly, you won't make it past this step. You must follow the print facility's instructions exactly. If they want a PDFx1a:2001 PDF file, do not upload a Press Quality PDF. You'll be dealing with random errors that will make you tear your hair out before you realize all the errors disappear when you upload the correct file type.

Most major print facilities offer a guide to help with the setup of the final files. Amazon KDP has an extensive online help section that covers file setup, and IngramSpark has a downloadable File Creation Guide PDF. Read these documents before creating your final files or share them with your designer if that person is not familiar with them. This single step will save you a lot of headaches. I've lost track of how many times in Facebook groups I've answered questions with direct quotes from the above sources and the frustrated author replies with

"Oh, I didn't know that." Read the print facility's guide. For those in the back, let me repeat that. Read the guides.

During the validation process, any number and variety of errors can occur. It's impossible to cover all within this book. However, some common errors are...

1. Size
   VERIFY THAT THE BOOK dimensions in your file match the trim size you chose under "Print Information/Details." If your book dimensions are 5x8, but you accidentally chose the trim size of 5.25x8 from the drop-down menu, you will receive an error. The simple fix is to return to the Print Details screen and adjust the trim size.

   Verify that your cover dimensions include the proper bleed. Remember, cover art dimensions are always slightly larger than the trim size.

   On KDP, the Bleed or No Bleed options for the interior pages can return errors depending on which option you chose. If you chose No Bleed and you have images or artwork that extend to the edge of the page, you will receive an error. To fix the problem, either reduce the dimensions of the image or artwork so it's within your page margins or add bleed to your document and extend the image to the outside edge of the bleed. Another error occurs if you chose Bleed but did not enlarge your page size to accommodate the extra amount of space around the page edges. To fix this, expand your page dimensions and extend your artwork to the outside edge.

2. Fonts
   FONTS MUST BE EMBEDDED in the PDF files. If you create the correct type of PDF, your fonts should automatically embed in the file. If you receive a font error, check the PDF type. If the type is correct, verify that the settings for creating the PDF did not change. For more information about embedding fonts, see Chapter 18: Final Print Submission Files.

3. Images
   IMAGES AND ARTWORK SOMETIMES create errors related to image resolution, image size, or color. Images in print books should

have a minimum resolution of 300 dpi. Anything less may cause poor reproduction on the printed page. If your book is in black-and-white, do not include color images in your PDF. The images must be grayscale. If your book is in color, your images need to be CMYK, not RGB.

4.  Page spreads
    WHILE IT'S NICE TO view book pages side-by-side on the screen, most print facilities require the PDF to be single pages, not page spreads. Submitting a PDF with page spreads will not give you the desired result. Check the correct option—spreads or single pages—when you export the PDF.

# 31
# DIGITAL PROOFS

WHEN YOU REACH THE proof stage, you are close to holding your printed book in your hand!

Once you upload your final files to the print facility, the facility will validate your files. After the files are validated, the electronic proof is issued in twenty-four to seventy-two hours, depending on the facility. You will receive an email that states your proof is available and asks you to sign in to your account to view the proof.

If the submitted files were set up correctly, you won't notice much difference between the files you submitted and the electronic proof. The proof will be a PDF that you can view on screen or download. If you've made previous arrangements with your designer, you can email the downloaded proof to them so they can check it.

Even though your submitted file and the proof look similar, you still need to carefully review the proof. Facilities often include instructions with the proof as to what specific items you should pay careful attention to.

After you review the proof, return to the link the facility sent to either accept or reject the proof.

# What to Check For

## Cover

VERIFY THAT THE COVER—FRONT and back—is correct. Make sure that nothing important is missing. The spine should look exactly how you want it, and neither front nor back cover imagery should overlap on the spine.

## Interior

1. Page position

   YOU PROBABLY SUBMITTED A PDF with the book as single pages. Your electronic proof may be single pages or spreads, depending on your settings in Adobe Acrobat Reader or a similar program. Ideally, you want to view the proof as spreads to verify the correct pages are side by side. How the pages appear as spreads is exactly how the book will print.

   If your proof is not in spreads, be careful if you change the PDF Page Display to Two Page View or a similar option. The first page of a book should be on the right-hand side; however, choosing Two Page View sometimes places that page on the left, which means the spreads will not be accurate. You can correct the spreads by choosing Show Cover Page in Two Page View from the Page Display options.

   The title page, table of contents, and the first page of the first chapter should be on the right-hand side of the spread. If any of these are out of place, you need to reject the proof and upload a corrected file. (Again, make sure you are viewing the PDF correctly.) If you planned on all chapters starting on the right-hand side of the spread, verify this and correct your original file if necessary.

2. Page numbering

   ODD NUMBERS SHOULD BE on the right and even numbers on the left. If your numbering is not correct, go back to your original manuscript file and adjust the numbering.

## Images

CAREFULLY CHECK ANY IMAGES or graphics. They should be clear, not fuzzy, on the electronic proof. Make sure they are lined up correctly with the text. If any are set to bleed off the page, check that nothing important will be cut off.

## Accept or Reject the Proof

AFTER YOU HAVE CAREFULLY reviewed the electronic proof, you have the option to accept or reject the proof. Do not accept the proof if you need to make corrections. Go back to your original file, make the corrections, export to a PDF again, and re-upload the file. The file will be validated again, and you will receive another electronic proof in twenty-four to seventy-two hours.

If you make corrections to the cover, you do not need to re-upload the interior file (unless you made corrections to it). The same goes for the interior: If you made changes to the interior and the cover is okay, upload the interior file only.

**TIP**

Name your PDF with the date or a version number so you know which file is the most recent and up-to-date.

### IngramSpark

IF YOU NEED TO make changes after viewing the electronic proof, do not approve the proof. If the proof is approved and then you upload new files, you will incur a $25 revision fee. Rejecting the proof and then uploading corrected files does not incur a fee. You can reject and upload as many times as necessary. However, once you accept the proof, any changes after that will incur the revision fee.

After accepting the proof, IngramSpark's system will ask if you want to keep the book private (only you can purchase copies) or if you want to enable distribution (make it available for anyone to purchase). Choose the private option if you want a printed proof of your book. To purchase a proof, go to the Order screen and place an order for one copy of your book. You will pay the production cost of your book plus shipping. Unfortunately, there's no guarantee as to how long the printed proof will take to arrive. If you are facing a deadline, you may want to skip the printed proof stage.

Information on how to order a printed proof from Amazon KDP is available here: kdp.amazon.com/en_US/help/topic/G202131440.

# 32

# FINAL
## STEPS

ONCE YOU APPROVE THE electronic proof, your book is ready for the next step. At an offset print facility, the book enters the physical production stage where your books are printed and shipped to you.

On Amazon KDP, the book goes live on the website within seventy-two hours.

At IngramSpark, new titles approved for distribution generally enter the distribution network at the end of the week, and it takes anywhere from twenty-four hours to approximately two months until your book appears on all the online retailer websites. Amazon typically picks up new titles from IngramSpark within twenty-four hours of when IngramSpark releases the title.

As your book enters the distribution network, the listings may appear wonky at first. Common problems include a missing book description, no cover or the wrong cover, no information at all other than a cover and title, and more. If one retailer has the correct, complete listing and another does not, do not panic. The retailer with the accurate listing tells you the information is correct and available. Give the other listings a couple of days to update. If you find an error in your listing, e.g., a misspelling in your book description, go to your dashboard and make the correction. IngramSpark pushes out the correct information when the various retailers check for updates.

## Corrections on a Live Book

WITH POD PRINTING, AFTER you approve the proof and your book is live, you can make corrections to your book at any time. The process for submitting corrections is the same—upload the revised file, wait for the electronic proof, and accept the proof. However, proceed with caution when making corrections. As I previously mentioned, at IngramSpark, anytime you upload a revised file, you will pay a $25 revision fee. (Amazon KDP and other facilities do not charge a revision fee.) Depending on the type of revision you make, your book may be listed as "temporarily unavailable" until it goes through the approval process again.

**TIP**

Some retailers pull a book's information from the ISBN agency. If a retailer has an older version of your cover or the image is missing, check the ISBN information on the ISBN's agency's website and update the cover image as necessary. You can also check bookwire.com to verify the listing is correct.

Once the revised book is approved and live, the new version is distributed to retailers, but the customer might still receive the old version. The retailer must sell all in-stock copies of the book before the new version is available. But if it is POD, why is there stock? Think about the following scenario.

Teresa's book is distributed to Amazon via IngramSpark. She launches her book, and it's climbing the rankings in her categories. Amazon's system recognizes the interest in the book and the influx of orders. So instead of ordering just one book to fulfill an order, Amazon might order a batch of twenty-five to match the demand expectations. The orders continue coming in for a day or two and then fizzle out. Now, Amazon has three of the twenty-five books left on a shelf in a warehouse. Unfortunately, some of Teresa's astute readers pointed out a glaring error in her book. She makes the correction and uploads a revised file to IngramSpark. Even though a revised version of Teresa's book is available, the next three people to order from Amazon will receive the old version of her book because those copies were already on Amazon's warehouse shelves. The fourth person to order will receive the revised version.

What do you do if the revision is critical? First, you could attempt to buy all the copies in the warehouse. However, if your book is distributed via Ingram, it's hard to say which retailers stocked the book, so you won't know where to purchase the old version from. Second, if the revision meets the requirements for a new ISBN, you could unpublish the old version and publish the revised version as a second edition or a new title. However, in that situation, you will likely lose any reviews and sales rankings. Both Amazon and IngramSpark have been cracking down on those who unpublish and re-publish the same book as a new title. Third, you could update your book description with a note that revisions have been made. If you only have a few revisions, you could include those directly in the book description.

# Sales Reporting

EVERY MONTH, ONLINE RETAILERS and distributors issue sales reports. These reports can be found via your account dashboard.

Unfortunately, the reports do not reveal details about who purchased your book. You will not know the buyer's age bracket, location, contact information, or any other information that might be useful for building a targeted advertising campaign. In fact, reports from distributors don't even show sales by retailer.

### To view reports on KDP and Draft2Digital:

1. Sign in to your account.
2. Click on the report option.
3. Once the sales dashboard loads, choose the activity and reports you want to view.

## To view reports on IngramSpark:

1. Sign in to your IngramSpark account.

2. On a computer, look at the navigation bar on the left. On a mobile device, tap the menu option.

3. Click on "Reports."

4. You'll see options for ebook and print sales, compensation, pre-orders, and financial reports.

5. Choose the report you want and enter the required information to generate the report.

# Payments

PAYMENT FOR SALES VIA online retailers and distributors is made sixty to ninety days after the end of the month when the sale was reported. For example, if KDP sold five copies of your book in January, you would receive payment sixty days later in late March or early April depending on KDP's payment schedule. Retailers have a window of time to report a sale to IngramSpark. This window allows for returns made to the retailer. Once the retailer reports the sale to IngramSpark, the sixty days start. So, if a customer purchased your book in May and the retailer reported the sale in June, you would receive payment the first week of September. Ebooks take about thirty days longer than print books for payment.

# 33
## YOU DID IT

CONGRATULATIONS! YOU'VE MADE IT through this book and are hopefully well on your way to becoming a self-published author. As you continue on your journey, remember to take one step at a time.

While I've tried to cover the basics of self-publishing, it's impossible to cover every scenario. If you come across something you do not understand or are unsure of, ask questions and do some research. The help sections for KDP and Ingram-Spark are full of trustworthy information related to self-publishing. Most service providers are willing to answer quick questions as part of their consultation process. Personally, I offer fifteen- and thirty-minute consultations as well as strategy sessions to help answer questions and plan self-publishing journeys. Facebook has a number of helpful self-publishing and writers' groups

### AUTHOR CENTRAL

Be sure to set up your Author Page and claim your books on Amazon KDP's Author Central. It's a great way for readers to connect with you and view your backlist (books you previously published).

where service providers hang out and answer questions. Before following the advice given in the answers, verify that the individual answering is a professional and experienced in publishing. Otherwise, you may receive incorrect advice and create more work for yourself in the long run.

As much as we all would love to sit back and let our books sell themselves, marketing and advertising are important parts of a book's journey. A book requires a long-term investment, but if done correctly, that investment will reap rewards. If you are just starting out and need help with advertising, I highly recommend Dave Chesson's Free Amazon Ads Course (kindlepreneur.com/free-amazon-ads-course/) and Mark Dawson's Ads for Authors (learn.selfpublishingformula.com/p/adsforauthors).

Self-publishing is an exciting journey, and the outcome of your journey is up to you. You've got this. Now, go publish that book!

**TIP**

Want to know which online retailers who are selling your book? Go to bookfinder.com and enter your ISBN. Note that not all retailers will be listed, but it should give you an idea.

# Three-Month Plan

My Target Book Launch Date: _____

USE THIS CHECKLIST TO keep your book on track for publication. Always consult your editor(s), designer(s), and print facilities for their timelines. It is possible to publish a book in three months or less, but it is 100% dependent on production schedules.

DON'T FORGET TO START planning your Book Launch Party!

## At Least Three Months before Launch

YOU WILL WANT TO take these steps before setting your target launch date since your choices of editor, designer, and print facilities may affect scheduling. For instance, your editor may have a full schedule, so the editing process may take ten weeks instead of the typical four to six weeks. In addition, some print companies have a turn-around time of a few days while others take longer, so plan accordingly.

- ❑ Interview book editors.
- ❑ Request a manuscript critique.
- ❑ Hire an editor.
- ❑ Prepare the final draft and send it to the editor.
- ❑ Establish your publishing company name.
- ❑ Hire a logo designer for your publishing company (optional).
- ❑ Assemble cover ideas and samples that you like.
- ❑ Research print facilities and distribution options.

# Three Months before Launch

WHILE THE EDITOR IS editing your manuscript, take the following steps.

## Week 1:

- ❑ Research, interview, and hire a cover designer.
- ❑ Hire a photographer to take your author photo.
- ❑ Write the book blurb.
- ❑ Write a short and long version of the author biography.

## Week 2:

- ❑ Write the book dedication and acknowledgments.
- ❑ Write the book description.
- ❑ Provide the cover designer with your author photo, book blurb, a brief author biography, and printing specifications.

## Week 3:

- ❑ Establish your author platform on any social media: Facebook, Instagram, Pinterest, and Twitter.
- ❑ Create a separate Facebook author page.
- ❑ Create a website or hire a website designer to do it for you.

## Week 4:

- ❑ Review edits from the editor and return the manuscript to the editor.
- ❑ Purchase the ISBN(s).
- ❑ Catch up on any details from previous weeks.

# Two Months before Launch

IN ADDITION TO FINALIZING edits, do the following.

## Week 1:

- ❑ Start advertising your upcoming book on social media.
- ❑ Interview and hire the interior page designer.
- ❑ Research pricing for all formats (print, ebook, and audio).

## Week 2:

- ❑ Finalize the cover design.
- ❑ Research the BISAC codes.
- ❑ Research metadata, keywords, and Amazon categories.

## Week 3:

- ❑ Review and authorize the final edited manuscript.
- ❑ Send the final version of the manuscript to your interior designer (include all front and back matter).
- ❑ Do a cover reveal on social media (optional).

## Week 4:

- ❑ Review the proofs of the interior page design.
- ❑ Assign the ISBN at myidentifiers.com.
- ❑ Request a LCCN from the Library of Congress
- ❑ Register the copyright.
- ❑ Send the ISBN barcode and the cover template from the print facility to cover designer.

# One Month before Launch

THE FOLLOWING STEPS NEED to take place in order for your book to be ready to print. Ideally, you want to accomplish these steps early in the month, preferably in weeks 1 and 2, although the physical printed proof may not arrive within that timeframe.

- ❑ Authorize the interior pages.
- ❑ Authorize the final cover.
- ❑ Send the final edited manuscript to the ebook creator unless you plan to do it yourself.
- ❑ Upload the print files to the printing company.
- ❑ Review the digital page proofs from the print facility.
- ❑ Review and authorize physical proof (optional).
- ❑ Order your author copies.

# Launch Day

Celebrate and enjoy your book launch day!

# Resources*

### Still have concerns about hiring an editor?
Read the book *Find a Real Editor: Avoiding the Posers and Scammers* by Jennifer Harshman. The book contains chapters full of advice from seven different editors.

### Need extra help with the self-publishing process?
Go to mountaincreekbooks.com to see the coaching, strategy, and design options I offer.

### Publishing a children's book?
Check out brookevitale.com/blog. Brooke offers insight and tons of tips for publishing picture books.

### Creating a full cover wrap in Canva?
Visit vaniamargene.com/2021/06/24/doing-a-full-paperback-wrap-in-canva-for-kdp-print-plus-screen-grabs/ for instructions on how to set up your file correctly.

### Struggling with marketing?
Pick up Craig Martelle's five book series Successful Indie Author and Shayla Raquel's book *The 10 Commandments of Author Branding*.

### Want an Index?
Search the American Society of Indexers at asindexing.org/find-an-indexer/ to locate a skilled indexer.

*All websites listed above and in this book were accurate at the time of publishing. The books listed are available on Amazon.

## About the Author

KARA STARCHER has worked as a freelance editor and book coach for almost two decades. She holds a bachelor's degree in Publishing and has spent time in the classroom teaching high school English. She calls the Appalachian Mountains in central West Virginia home. Visit her website at mountaincreekbooks.com.

Made in the USA
Monee, IL
17 April 2022

94879339R00105